The Taxi Project

The Taxi Project:
Realistic Solutions for Today

Edited by Emilio Ambasz
Project Director

**With essays by
Emilio Ambasz
G. N. Georgano
Brian Richards
Martin Wohl**

The Museum of Modern Art
New York

Copyright © 1976
by The Museum of Modern Art
All rights reserved
Library of Congress Catalog Card Number 76-1493
ISBN 0-87070-277-7

Cover design: Emilio Ambasz
Book design: April Greiman
Type set by Boro Typographers, Inc.
New York, N.Y.
Printed by Eastern Press, Inc.
New Haven, Conn.

The Museum of Modern Art
11 West 53 Street
New York, N.Y. 10019
Printed in the United States of America

The Taxi Project exhibition, shown at The Museum of Modern Art, New York, from June 17, 1976, to September 6, 1976, has been made possible by grants from the Urban Mass Transportation Administration of the United States Department of Transportation and the Mobil Oil Corporation.

Co-sponsors of this exhibition are the Taxi and Limousine Commission of New York City, the New York City Taxi Drivers' Union (Local 3036, AFL-CIO), and the International Taxicab Association.

Table of Contents

Acknowledgments

The Taxi Project: Realistic Solutions for Today was first conceived in 1973, but intensive work began only in May, 1974, after a number of administrative and financial problems had been resolved. These years have been the most profoundly critical and decisive in the automobile industry since its beginnings. To bring this project to a satisfactory conclusion required the understanding and support of innumerable organizations. The preparation of the prototypes in the exhibition demanded the imagination and resources of literally hundreds of people in Europe and the United States: the executives of the automobile companies who responded to the Museum's invitation to submit prototypes; the engineers and designers who conceived them; the test drivers and researchers who checked them; the graphic designers and photographers who illustrated their documentation; the liaison officers within each company who coordinated their work. There are also a host of others in administrative positions—though they must remain anonymous here—whose indispensable assistance was greatly appreciated.

On behalf of the Trustees of The Museum of Modern Art, I wish to express particular gratitude to the Urban Mass Transportation Administration of the United States Department of Transportation and to the Mobil Oil Corporation for the generous support they have given to this project from its inception. Special recognition is due to Herbert Schmertz, Vice President for Public Affairs of Mobil, for his fine comprehension of the meaning and impact that this show would have for urban transportation. His deep sense of cultural and social commitment honors the organization he serves. Dr. Wilhelm Raithel of the Urban Mass Transportation Administration provided intellectual support, and also great assistance in negotiating the maze of bureaucratic procedures.

Within the participating automobile companies we would like to thank Pehr G. Gyllenhammar, President of the Volvo group, for his clear and forceful vision of the project's potential for industry and the community, and Robert Dethorey, General Manager of Volvo's Car Division, who was instrumental in obtaining Volvo's enthusiastic support for this project. To both we express our admiration for their enlightened recognition of the automobile industry's responsibilities in solving our cities' traffic problems. A special note of acknowledgment is due to Dr. Rolf Mellde, Director of Advanced Engineering of Volvo, who guided the company's engineering, mechanical, and design efforts. Among the many competent members of Volvo's team we would like to mention: Raymond Eknor, Senior Project Engineer; Jan Wilsgaard, Chief Designer; and Michel Naert and Leif Osterholm, Project Engineers. Dan Werbin, Manager of Product Development of Volvo of America Corporation, and responsible for liaison between Volvo and The Museum of Modern

Art, greatly deserves our thanks for his efficient and resourceful cooperation.

Professor Ernst Fiala, Volkswagen's Vice President of Research and Development, merits our recognition for his understanding of the possibilities that taxis offer as testing ground for difficult traffic conditions, and for his support of this project's objectives. Dr. Ing. Wolfgang Lincke, Volkswagen's Director of Research, provided enlightened guidance and deserves our special gratitude. Special notes of acknowledgment are due to Dr. Harald Schimkat, Manager, Automobile and Traffic Technology Research Department, who enthusiastically assumed direct responsibility for producing Volkswagen's prototype, and to Dr. A. Kalberlah, Volkswagen's Manager, Traffic Technology Section, as well as to the members of their team for their brilliant contributions to the development of Volkswagen's hybrid-propulsion engine. The following officers in Volkswagen of America, Inc., were also extremely helpful: Arthur R. Railton, Vice President; Joseph Kennebeck, Manager, Emissions, Safety, and Development Department; Chester Bahn, Manager, Public Information Department; and Lawrence Fabbro, of Lawrence Associates, consultant to Volkswagen. We are very grateful for their cordial and competent help.

In thanking the Department of Transportation we wish not only to indicate our gratitude for support of the Taxi Project, but to acknowledge their commitment to underwrite the production of the exhibition's two American prototypes. We also wish to recognize the full cooperation of Alan Roth, Vice President and General Manager of American Machine and Foundry Advanced Systems Laboratory, Santa Barbara, California and William Wingenbach, Director of Advanced Engineering; and of Richard D. Burtz, General Manager, Steam Power Systems, San Diego, California.

We are also grateful to Alfa Romeo for making available, *hors concours,* the taxi prototype they are developing on their own for the Italian and European market. The prototype will not be tested, like the other four, after the exhibition, by the New York City Taxi and Limousine Commission (TLC) and will not be manufactured in the United States. However, Alfa Romeo decided to create their prototype using the guidelines established by our Design Specifications Manual.

Bruce McWilliams of British Leyland Motors, USA, merits particular recognition for his solicitous help and his unflagging enthusiasm for this project. We are thankful to Lawrence Gang for lending us his own London taxi for the duration of the show.

We are much obliged to Michael J. Lazar, former Chairman of the New York City Taxi and Limousine Commission, and to Moses L. Kove, the present Chairman, who warmly endorsed the

Taxi Project. Within the Commission we are thankful to Alex Mautner, former Director of the Department of Technical Control, for his skillful guidance through the intricacies of city government. We are obliged to Ronald Adams, Technical Consultant to the Commission, for his role in the preparation of the Design Specification Manual, and for his continued intellectual concern for this project.

The historical and critical essays contained in this publication were the responsibility of G. N. Georgano, Martin Wohl, and Brian Richards, to whom we are most grateful for their incisive and thoughtful contributions. We are also thankful to *Technology Review,* edited at the Massachusetts Institute of Technology, for permission to preprint Martin Wohl's essay "Increasing the Taxi's Role in Urban America" (copyright 1976 by the Alumni Association of M.I.T.).

During the many months I spent organizing this project, I met cordial cooperation from far more people than can be enumerated here. But I must mention my gratitude to Robert Rickles of the Institute for Public Transportation for his opportune and thoughtful advice. William Ritman's experience in stage design and his helpful suggestions on my exhibition layout were invaluable. I am similarly indebted to Karl Ludwigsen, automotive engineer and consultant to this museum, for his advice during the preparation of the Design Specifica-

tions Manual. I am most grateful to Michael Sorkin for assisting in the initial stages of the Taxi Project.

I am indebted in many ways to numerous colleagues at the Museum. Richard Palmer, Coordinator of Exhibitions, patiently and competently steered the show through complicated administrative procedures. Nancy Englander, formerly of the Museum's development office, was of invaluable assistance in obtaining the cooperation of our sponsors. Elizabeth Shaw, Director of the Department of Public Information, and Linda Gordon, Associate Director, resourcefully concerned themselves with the publicity for this show. Jeanne Thayer, Chairman of the Special Events Program, assumed responsibility for ensuring the gracious and earnest expression of the Museum's gratitude to the sponsors of the exhibition and the representatives of the participating companies. To Jeanne Thayer, Lee Granger, the members of Lee Granger's committee, and Sarah Hoge, I am most grateful.

Pat White served as editor of the publication during its most decisive phases. To Margaret Sheffield, who served as editor during the production phase, I wish to express appreciation for her professional standards and her devotion to the task. With good humor, Francis Kloeppel, Managing Editor, and Jack Doenias, Production Manager, exerted special efforts to meet a particularly

arduous production schedule without
loss of quality.

Manuel Yanez concerned himself with
the construction details of the installation of the show. April Greiman,
Graphic Design Consultant, collabo-
rated with professional competence and
inordinate patience.

The handsome drawings illustrating
examples of historical taxicabs were
executed for the exhibition by Donald
Wieland of Quinlan Artwork, to whom
we are much obliged. The alpha-
numerical Self-Scan electronic display
system at the exhibition was generously
provided by Burroughs Corporation,
Federal and Special Systems Group,
to whom we owe a debt of gratitude.

Within my own department of Architecture and Design, I wish to express
my thanks to Katherine Mansfield, my
former assistant, for her unflagging
enthusiasm and tactful advice, and to
my present assistant, Marie-Anne Evans,
for her most skillful help and thorough
cooperation. I am especially grateful to
Arthur Drexler both for his most enthusiastic support of this project and
for his encouragement throughout its
development.

Emilio Ambasz

The Taxi Project:
Prototypes

Introduction

milio Ambasz

Taxis are the unsung heroes of urban transportation. Their industry is an important part of the national transit system, and a key factor in intra-urban movement. In the United States some 170,000 taxis serve 2.5 billion passengers yearly in more than 3400 communities and generate 2.2 billion dollars in gross revenues. In New York City alone, taxis move 800,000 passengers per day and produce a greater revenue than that of the Metropolitan Transit Authority.

In the United States, the standard 6-passenger sedan is the vehicle typically chosen for taxi service. While better suited to family use in suburban and rural areas, this vehicle is unsatisfactory for taxi service in congested urban environments. For over half its service time the cab is occupied by the driver alone, and typical customer occupancy, in New York City for example, is on the order of 1.5 persons. From the economic and ecological point of view, such a mismatch of transport capability to actual payload is a crucial problem. This problem is compounded by high emission rates and high energy consumption in relation to actual payload moved, and by the spatial requirements for storing and moving such oversized vehicles in a space-limited environment. The taxi vehicle appears to be the only urban "transit" vehicle which is not expressly designed for its particular type of service.

Recognizing the critical requirements of public urban mobility and the absence of appropriately designed automotive means to satisfy such needs, The

Museum of Modern Art, New York, through its Department of Architecture and Design, proposed and organized the Taxi Project. With this in mind, the Taxi and Limousine Commission of New York City, in close collaboration with the Museum's staff and its engineering consultants, and in consultation with the representatives of New York City taxi fleet owners and private taxi owners, prepared a Design Specifications Manual for a new urban vehicle which might serve as a taxi. (See pages 93–104.)

Since the Museum's goal was not to engage in an academic exercise but rather to obtain the cooperation of the automobile industry in producing actual working prototypes which could be tested by professional taxi drivers in American cities, independent designers and schools of design were not consulted. In all cases, the Museum stressed a pragmatic approach. The aim was to achieve a realistically designed vehicle which could be produced at a reasonable price, and which would better serve the needs of the taxi industry, the driver, and the passengers.

The Museum has had a long history, dating back to 1936, of working together with industry and government to improve the quality of industrial and architectural design, and to raise the level of public awareness regarding the problems and potentialities of our environment. Many classics of contemporary design, such as the chairs designed by Charles Eames and Eero Saarinen, have been the result of competitions and exhibitions organized by the Museum's

Department of Architecture and Design. Experience has shown that this form of cooperation has made it possible for many new design ideas to enter the public consciousness and become a material reality.

The Museum sought the widest American participation for the Taxi Project. Ford, General Motors, Chrysler, and American Motors were approached first; other American manufacturers later approached included Mack Trucks and Checker Motors, companies directly engaged in vehicle production; the rest were major American corporations, in various ways concerned with engine and/or agricultural and construction vehicle design (Westinghouse, General Electric, Grumman, International Harvester, Cummins Engine, Deere, White Motor, etc). All declined to participate. Consequently, the U.S. Department of Transportation, through its Urban Mass Transportation Administration (UMTA), made funds available—through an open-bid competition—for two American companies that would create a low-pollution taxi vehicle. This vehicle, which UMTA calls a paratransit vehicle, had to fulfill the requirements of the Design Specifications Manual. American Machine and Foundry, Inc. (AMF), and Steam Power Systems, Inc. (SPS), each won a contract. In addition, the Museum decided to invite European manufacturers who would commit themselves to mass-produce such a taxi in the United States if the market proved satisfactory. Volvo, now building an assembly plant in Chesapeake, Virginia, and Volkswagen, expecting to have a

factory in America before 1980, accepted the Museum's invitation. A third European company, Alfa Romeo, adopted the Museum's Design Specifications for developing—on its own—a taxi for the European market; the Alfa prototype is also being exhibited in the Taxi Project.

Even allowing for the troubled state of the economy in the period 1974–75 and the many problems now facing the automobile industry, the negative decision of the American manufacturers seems shortsighted. Since their conclusions were not shared by two of their European competitors, it is possible to draw unfavorable inferences from the reluctance of the American automobile industry to confront what others regard as an opportunity for social benefits and financial rewards.

Among the factors the participants were asked to consider in designing their working prototypes were the safety and comfort of the driver, ease of communication with passenger, and ease of loading and unloading baggage. From the point of view of fleet owners, the new designs were to be more efficient and economical to operate and maintain. From the point of view of the passenger, they were to be more comfortable and efficient, roomy enough to allow entrance for a mother with a baby carriage or a handicapped person in a wheelchair. From the point of view of the city, the prototypes had to be designed with the objective of significantly reducing pollution and traffic congestion. The pronounced height and squareness of the vehicles in the Taxi Project exhibition are the consequence of the extremely rigorous requirements and restrictions set by the Design Specifications Manual.

The Museum devised two methods of approach for the design and development of a new taxi. The first approach entailed developing vehicles designed and built completely from scratch. The second represents the other end of the spectrum, that is to say, utilizing off-the-shelf components. The prototypes developed by Volvo, American Machine and Foundry, and Steam Power Systems correspond to the first approach (see technical description in their respective sections). The taxi design presented by Volkswagen answers to the premises of the second.

American Machine and Foundry and Steam Power Systems produced, under contract to the Department of Transportation, one prototype each, both of which operate on steam-powered propulsion plants. The level of pollution of such open combustion chamber type of motors is very low. Also new are the body designs and the interior features. Volvo's prototype is based on a specially developed diesel engine; diesel engines have proven to conform with the existing exhaust emission requirements by a good margin. The chassis, body, and interior of the vehicle are also new designs. One interesting feature of the Volvo prototype is that it can be extended to become a maxi-taxi for nine passengers. Volkswagen based its design on an existing vehicle, the VW Station Wagon, which it adapted for taxi use by redesigning the interior facilities for passengers and driver, and by introducing features intended to make the vehicle more easily accessible. Volkswagen's important contribution to the problem of designing an urban vehicle suitable for taxi use is the introduction of a hybrid power plant—the combination of an electric motor and an internal combustion engine—which produces no exhaust emission when operated electrically at the low speeds that city traffic often necessitates. (For further discussion see the essays and detailed descriptions which the engineering and design teams of each of the companies have supplied to accompany the presentation of their respective taxi prototypes.)

At the beginning of this project the Museum searched for advanced propulsion systems that would not contribute to polluting the atmosphere and would not squander precious and dwindling resources. It soon became evident that electrically driven motors, in addition to still requiring heavy batteries, have not yet solved their major problem: replenishing their power supply. This requires, so far, that electricity be generated by a prohibitively expensive use of energy sources, such as gasoline. Hydroelectric and solar energy, although their possibilities are boundless, have yet to be developed into the economical power sources we hope the future will provide us.

The taxi vehicles presented at the Museum have successfully answered many of the very rigorous requirements set by the Design Specifications Manual.

They represent what is feasible today within the constraints of the present economy. They are practical and realistic solutions that industry can produce at reasonable prices and that can be operated economically. These taxis, specially designed for meeting urban traffic conditions, might considerably improve the quality of life in the urban environment, for they would use less energy, reduce air pollution, and cut traffic congestion, as well as provide safe and comfortable accommodations for passengers and luggage. It is hoped that the Taxi Project will promote the manufacture and introduction of a more suitable taxicab vehicle before the end of this decade. Taxicabs are not the panacea for the problems of mass transportation, but, as this project shows, they can go a long way toward providing us today with better urban transportation. This is no small contribution toward ensuring that our cities have a future.

The possibilities for the future of urban and suburban transportation by means of taxis are greatly broadened by the fact that the Urban Mass Transportation Administration of the U.S. Department of Transportation is now seriously exploring the possibilities for public transportation offered by para-transit systems, which comprise (in addition to standard taxis) jitneys, dial-a-ride, subscription services, and similar setups. By means of research contracts and demonstration grants—such as the one under which the two American entries to the Taxi Project were developed—the Department of Transportation is attempting to prove the potential of taxis in public transpor-

tation. It is to be fervently hoped that DOT's enlightened leadership will help bring about legislation providing independent taxi owners and fleet operators with financial facilities for acquiring specially developed taxi vehicles like those here presented. In another important area of public-transportation financing, Federal grants might well be made available to private taxi groups interested in developing new and better types of taxi services. Only then will para-transit assume to the full the public-transportation role it has gallantly proven—under adverse conditions—to be capable of.

It is the declared intention of the New York City Taxi and Limousine Commission to test the submitted prototypes. Those prototype vehicles found suitable for the rigorous demands of taxi service will be used in evolving standards for all future taxicab designs approved for use in New York City. It is under the actual conditions of taxi service, therefore, that the Commission will carry out the testing and field demonstration of accepted prototypes resulting from the Taxi Project.

Emilio Ambasz
Curator of Design
Director of the Taxi Project

Department of Transportation

The Para-Transit Vehicle Project
Between private passenger cars and standard public transit vehicles there exists a wide range of urban vehicles, vans, and taxis which are used to provide various urban transportation services. This type of service, called para-transit, provides an alternate to individual passenger car use and ownership, and it is of vital importance to people without ready access to regular mass transit and to the 13 million elderly and handicapped persons of limited mobility. In addition, para-transit aids fixed-route bus and rail service lines by providing feeder service, which, in effect, increases patronage and extends the area served. Most para-transit vehicles, however, were not designed nor optimized for the services in which they are used.

The majority of taxicabs, which constitute the largest percentage of para-transit vehicles, are slightly modified private passenger automobiles, designed primarily with appearance in mind rather than functional considerations. Trends in automobile design have exacerbated the problem. Over the last 10 to 20 years the design of passenger cars has become lower, sleeker, and perhaps more appealing to the eye, but the design has made it more difficult to get in and out of automobiles, particularly where the sidewalk is above average in elevation. Many elderly or physically handicapped persons find it difficult or impossible to use taxi service.

There are about 13 million elderly and handicapped persons in this country who find it difficult or impossible to use presently available mass transportation services and for whom today's taxicab in its most frequent models is not the solution, either. More than seven million of these elderly and handicapped persons are estimated to live in urban areas.

Concern for persons of limited mobility was expressed in the statement by the U.S. Congress in the Appropriations Committee's report of June 15, 1973, in which funds were provided "for the development of an improved, efficient, quiet, non-polluting taxi." This then became the start of the Para-Transit Vehicle Project by the U.S. Department of Transportation's Urban Mass Transportation Administration (UMTA).

UMTA is chartered to improve urban mass transportation through assistance to systems providing transit services, and it is required by law that the services resulting from this Federal assistance be available to all, including elderly and handicapped persons.

The development program for the para-transit vehicle focused on a small general-purpose, well-designed, highly functional urban transit vehicle that is more versatile than the typical taxicab. These design objectives included consideration of existing Federal statutes which would affect its use if it were put into manufacturing production. For example, at the time when the para-transit vehicle program was undertaken, the U.S. Environmental Protection Agency's regulations required all small passenger vehicles to be propelled by very low pollution engines by 1977. Thus, the

UMTA para-transit vehicle had to be designed to comply with that law.

Since total absence of pollution as a practical matter was beyond the limits of technology (and still is), UMTA specified that the vehicles had to meet the emission requirements initially mandated for 1977 and now postponed to 1978: CO–3.4, HC–0.41, and NO_x–0.40, all in grams per mile. It was realized that this was a very demanding requirement, and UMTA was willing to accept the best fuel efficiency and noise levels achievable under these constraints.

In March, 1975, UMTA awarded two contracts, one to AMF, Inc., Advanced Systems Laboratory in Santa Barbara, California, and another to Steam Power Systems in San Diego, California. Both companies proposed the use of steam engines in order to meet the stringent emission requirements. SPS offered an improved version of the engine Jay Carter Enterprises had developed and installed in a VW Squareback.

After their exhibition at The Museum of Modern Art, the two vehicles will be assigned to the Transportation Systems Center of the Department of Transportation in Cambridge, Massachusetts, and subjected there to a series of tests to determine and evaluate their performance characteristics. The International Taxicab Association has been asked to assess their suitability for taxicab service before the testing is initiated. UMTA is preparing a grant to ITA to provide funding for the conduct of its evaluation.

The present phase of the para-transit vehicle project establishes the feasibility and practicality of essentially three issues:

1 *Space Utilization:* A vehicle of sub-compact size can be designed to accommodate four passengers in comfort, one of them in a wheelchair.

2 *Accessibility:* A wheelchair passenger can board the vehicle without assistance, if he or she so desires.

3 *Emissions:* Such a vehicle can meet the most stringent emission standards without the use of catalytic mufflers and at fuel mileages equal to the average 1975 gasoline engine.

Thus, the vehicles were designed from inception as para-transit vehicles. They are not converted automobiles.

Although the para-transit vehicles procured by the Urban Mass Transportation Administration are engineering prototypes as contrasted to production prototypes, consideration is given in their design to volume production, maintainability, reliability, and other features which are important to assure wide acceptance by the para-transit industry. The vehicles are compact in size, with overall lengths of about 175 in. and overall widths of about 70 in., yet each has a spacious, comfortable, easily accessible interior. Overall height is 70 in., providing 58 in. of interior vertical space. Large glass areas and narrow pillars allow excellent visibility for both driver and passengers.

The primary passenger accommodation area has a flat 48 in. wide and 30 in. fore and aft. In its deployed position, the extra jump seat does not protrude into this area.

The effort needed for opening and closing the passenger doors is minimized so that most handicapped persons will be able to operate them without assistance. The exterior door controls are equipped with hold-open latches. The vehicle doors may be opened and closed by a system operated by the driver to permit ingress and egress for the wheelchair passenger, without the need for the driver to leave his seat. An ingress and egress ramp slope is less than 1 ft. per 12 ft.

While the driver is protectively isolated from the other occupants by a transparent partition, provisions are made to facilitate voice contact and fare transactions. This partition does not restrict driver or passenger egress in the event of emergency evacuation. Heating, air conditioning, and fresh air ventilation are provided for all vehicle occupants. Separate controls are provided for the passenger and driver compartments.

Special display conveniences and equipment include a door-ajar warning light, space for the driver's personal articles, space for a two-way radio fully operable from the driver's position with the driver's restraint device utilized. Provisions have been made for a fare-metering system to be easily accessible to the driver and its readout to be in full view of the forward-facing passengers.

The noise level inside the moving vehicle, with all windows closed, measured at the location of the passenger's head, meets standards at 30 mph and at 60 mph constant speed.

The vehicles also meet all applicable Federal Motor Vehicle Safety Standards (FMVSS), and amendments presently in effect, as well as all the applicable Motor Carrier Safety Regulations published by the Bureau of Motor Carrier Safety of the U.S. Federal Highway Administration.

In the interest of reducing vehicle repair costs and to minimize the likelihood of accidents while maneuvering in congested areas, the vehicle exterior corners, front and rear, incorporate the largest practical radius. The front of the body is curved, smooth, and free from hard edges and projections which might cause injuries to pedestrians.

Doors and quarter panels are designed to reduce body work and finish repair resulting from light to moderate side collisions with other vehicles.

Bumper coverage is between 12 in. and 20 in. above the road surface. The bumper face is a simple curvature. In addition, the bumpers incorporate two or more horizontal ridges running the length of the bumper, raised slightly beyond the bumper face itself. The bumpers also are basically flush with the quarter panel or fenders above them. They do not protrude excessively beyond the quarter panels in order to minimize potential for snagging other vehicles.

To obtain both a high degree of maneuverability and fuel economy, the vehicles are as light as feasible and have been designed to be small and to minimize aerodynamic drag. They can accelerate from 0 to 45 mph in 11 seconds. Designed as urban vehicles, they were not required to be able to exceed 65 mph. With their steam engines, they obtain a fuel mileage between 10 and 17 mpg over the Federal Urban Dynamometer Driving Test Cycle.

Contract requirements for engine performance are met, including very stringent emission standards, with the use of unleaded regular gasoline. These engines have been designed to be adaptable to use other fuels like diesel fuel, kerosene, and heating oil.

Operational handling of the para-transit vehicles is convenient and efficient. The minimum turning diameter of both is less than 35 ft., curb to curb. Vehicle stability and handling characteristics are comparable to those of current model compact cars.

Features and capabilities such as those enumerated here should make it possible to add a new dimension of mobility to those who find it difficult or impossible to use available transportation systems. It is difficult to assess the level of demand for the service that the new para-transit vehicles could provide, but the probability is high that, once this new type of conveyance is offered, a large number of people who now do not have adequate mobility will want to make use of such service.

The Para-Transit Vehicle Project is intended to serve as a step in this direction.

Urban Mass Transportation Administration
U.S. Department of Transportation

Department of Transportation:
AMF Taxi Prototype

Manufacturer	American Machine & Foundry, Advanced Systems Laboratory, Goleta, California	
Engine	2-cylinder steam engine (single-acting uniflow Carter Enterprises engine)	
	30 cu. in.	492 cu. cm.
	105 bhp at 5500 rpm	

Performance

Max. speed	75 mph	120 km./h
Acceleration	0 to 45 mph in 11 seconds	
Fuel consumption	17.5 mpg (city) 7.5 km./l.	
Fuel type	Unleaded gasoline, diesel fuel, kerosene, methanol, etc.	
Emission	Meets all present and proposed Federal emission standards	

Body frame	Unit steel/aluminum
Transmission	3-speed automatic
Drive	Front-wheel drive

Steering

Type	Rack and pinion	
Turn radius	17.5 ft.	5.25 m.

Braking system

front/rear	Disc/drum

Suspension

front/rear	Independent unequal-length arms/solid axle with trailing arms

Overall dimensions

Max. length	182.8 in.	457 cm.
Max. width	72 in.	180 cm.
Max. height	70 in.	175 cm.
Wheelbase	108 in.	270 cm.
Track front/rear	63 in./ 63 in.	160 cm./ 160 cm.

Interior dimensions
passenger compartment

Length	82 in.	208 cm.
Width	61 in.	155 cm.
Headroom over aisle	56 in.	142 cm.

Weight	3300 lb.	1485 kg.
Ground clearance	6.5 in.	16.5 cm.
Entry height	11 in.	28 cm.
General data	Carries 4 to 5 passengers plus driver; powered ramp for wheelchair; passenger sliding door; air-conditioned	

American Machine and Foundry

The vehicle which AMF's Advanced Systems Laboratory has produced for the U.S. Department of Transportation has been designed in response to the unique requirements of a para-transit vehicle. The services to be provided are of a mixed nature, with passengers ranging from one to five—able-bodied or handicapped—and trip lengths varying from a few blocks to tens of miles. Further, the vehicle must cope with extremes in weather, variations of road surfaces, and traffic. The car must also provide comfort and safety, must not pollute, and must be commercially viable.

Comfort and Convenience
Passenger visibility is extremely good. The interior is roomy and easily accessible. The vehicle is 70 in. (178 cm.) high in order to provide a full 58 in. (147.3 cm.) of interior space.

The rear roof incorporates an air exit, which in conjunction with environmental control equipment, provides air circulation within the passenger compartment.

Passenger-Driver Separation
The spacious, accessible driver's compartment is isolated from the passenger compartment by a bullet-resistant lower bulkhead and an upper transparent bullet-resistant barrier. The compartment contains all vehicle controls, a safe deposit compartment, communication equipment, engine monitoring instruments, fare meter, etc. The compartment is designed to provide a comfortable and safe environment for drivers of different sizes. The compartment and the driver are protected from crash injury by suitable restraints and by a structural front crash energy management system.

Accessibility
The large sliding rear doors are electrically unlatched and actuated. The doors swing outward to clear the body and glide rearward. In the event of power failure, the doors may be manually unlatched and opened from within. The open door provides an area large enough for the comfortable entry of the handicapped, including a person in a wheelchair. When open, the door un-

covers a pocket in the thick structural floor which houses a wheelchair ramp. This ramp can be extended to the right side of the vehicle to permit wheelchair entry. Ramp actuation is by electrical power. When the vehicle is in motion, the wheelchair will be secured, rear-facing, in the right side seat position.

Crash Safety

The front bumper is an aluminum structure attached to the vehicle with impact energy absorbing units. Attached to the bumper faces are horizontal elastomeric ribs to reduce bumper damage and to prevent bumper override or underride with another vehicle. Elastomeric side units connect the bumper to the side of the vehicle. The entire assembly is sufficiently pliable to prevent vehicle damage during low velocity impacts and to minimize injury to any pedestrians struck.

All front lights including the rectangular headlights are recessed into the sheet metal for maximum protection in case of frontal impacts.

Dimensions

The vehicle, which measures 182.8 in. (464.3 cm.) in overall length and 72 in. (183 cm.) in overall width, is compact in size, yet at the same time it is spacious and comfortable.

Driver Vision

The vehicle is simple and safe to maneuver. The short front overhang provides excellent forward visibility so that the driver can guide the vehicle in tight turns and difficult parking.

Design Safety Features

The right front hatch provides access to the environmental control equipment and can be used as an emergency entry or exit area from the driver's compartment.

The rear bumper treatment is the same as the front. There is sufficient pliability in the bumper assembly and associated body panels to resist damage during mild rear impacts.

The large rear window is oriented to avoid reflecting light toward drivers of following vehicles.

Body Design and Special Features

A large lightweight hood is provided to allow full access to the engine compartment and cowl-mounted hardware.

Windshield and side windows are large and flush-mounted to reduce wind noise. The lower side body panels are painted with an epoxy paint to minimize damage from pebbles and other objects, or from bumping into other vehicle doors. These side panels are easily removable to minimize repair costs after side collisions.

The two forward-facing, primary passenger seats are permanently installed over the rear axle area. The remainder of the rear compartment is convertible for use with a wheelchair plus two or three rear-facing passengers. Interior features include a cutaway roofline at the rear door openings which gives added headroom for ease of entry or exit. There is substantial structure in all roof support posts. The black color of

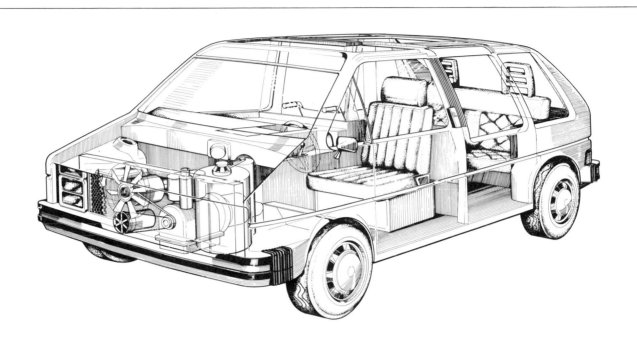

...rawing showing ...ont and side with ...arter steam engine ... front of vehicle.

...rawing showing ...de view indicating ...terior space and ...mp for wheelchair.

*Hood raised to show
placement of Jay
Carter Enterprises
steam engine.*

View of driver's compartment.

The AMF prototype with wheelchair ramp extended.
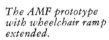

the rear "C" post reduces the appearance of massiveness in this area.

The vehicle body is fabricated mainly from automotive steel and aluminum in a manner similar to that used in conventional vehicles. The para-transit vehicle body components, however, were hand-formed rather than tool-formed.

A preliminary weight estimate of the vehicle is about 3300 lbs. (1485 kg.) curb weight.

Propulsion and Engine
After an exhaustive study of propulsion systems, the engine identified as satisfying AMF's needs for this vehicle was a Jay Carter Enterprises steam engine. This engine has the desirable features of low emissions, good fuel economy, multi-fuel capability, low weight, small volume, and suitable performance.
—**American Machine and Foundry**

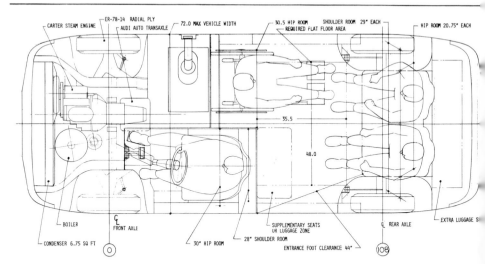

Elevation of AMF taxi indicating dimensions.

Plan of AMF taxi prototype.

Department of Transportation:
SPS Taxi Prototype

Manufacturer	Steam Power Systems, San Diego, California
Engine	4-cylinder steam engine (compound counterflow SPS engine) 148 cu. in. 2400 cu. cm. 66 bhp at 1000 rpm
Performance	
Max. speed	66 mph 105 km./h
Acceleration	0 to 60 mph in 15 seconds
Fuel consumption	12 mpg (city) 5.1 km./l.
Fuel type	Unleaded gasoline, diesel fuel, kerosene, methanol, etc.
Emission	Meets all present and proposed Federal emission standards
Body frame	Unibody (monocoque construction)
Transmission	2-speed automatic
Drive	Rear-wheel drive
Steering	
Type	Rack and pinion, unassisted
Turn radius	16 ft. 4.80 m.
Braking system	
front/rear	Disc/drum
Suspension	
front/rear	Torsion springs/torsion springs

Overall dimensions

Max. length	171 in.	427.5 cm.
Max. width	68 in.	170 cm.
Max. height	84 in.	210 cm.
Wheelbase	104 in.	260 cm.
Track	63 in./	160 cm./
front/rear	62 in.	157.5 cm.

Interior dimensions

passenger compartment

Length	61 in.	155 cm.
Width	62 in.	157.5 cm.
Headroom over aisle	61 in.	155 cm.

Weight	2950 lb.	1338 kg.
Ground clearance	6 in.	15 cm.
Entry height	12.5 in.	31.75 cm.
General data	Carries 2 passengers plus 1 passenger on wheelchair or 5 in squeeze loading; powered ramp for wheelchair; bifold hydraulic doors both sides, operated by passengers or driver; air-conditioned	

Steam Power Systems

The para-transit vehicle concept has emerged over the past several years to fill the gap between public mass transportation and the privately owned automobile in an urban environment. The purpose of this paper is to explain the approach taken by Steam Power Systems (SPS), Inc., in designing and producing an operating engineering prototype steam taxi.

Para-transit is defined to include all types of public transit between privately owned cars and scheduled rail, bus, and air service. The para-transit vehicle includes the taxicab, mini-bus, jitney, dial-a-ride, personal rapid transit, and dual mode systems. It provides an alternative to individual car ownership and use, and is of vital importance to people without ready access to regular mass transit and to people of limited mobility.

Vehicles presently available for para-transit service do not incorporate the full spectrum of characteristics required. Those used for most dial-a-ride applications are larger than needed. The great majority of taxicabs which form the bulk of present para-transit vehicles are slightly modified private passenger cars, designed more for appearance than for function.

The U.S. Department of Transportation (DOT) has funded the development of an engineering prototype to evaluate current technology.

Accommodations
Public acceptance of the SPS taxi prototype is contingent in part upon a high level of comfort and convenience for the paying passenger. The two primary passenger seats provide armchair-like dimensions and comfort, while the boxy overall configuration provides a feeling of interior space not possible in a conventionally spaced automobile. Complete climate control is provided. Separate vent, heat, and air conditioning controls are provided for driver and passenger compartments. The air conditioning load and outside glare are reduced by darkly tinted windows. Wheelchair-seated passengers are provided a wide, automatically operated door and ramp, and a separate restraint system which secures both passenger and wheelchair in a position against the left-side forward corner of the passenger compartment. Luggage is carried on board by the passengers themselves and stowed on the passenger compartment floor.

Dimensions
Vehicle size limitations imposed by DOT include an overall length of 190 in. (483 cm.) and width of 72 in. (183 cm.) with a target curb weight of 2950 lbs. (1338 kg.). As a comparison, the delivered vehicle will be shorter, narrower, and 200 lbs. (91 kg.) lighter than the 1975 Ford Mustang II V8. The turning circle is 32 ft. (9.8 m.), less than that of any 1975 VW.

Accessibility

The SPS taxi prototype provides for the ingress and egress of a wheelchair-seated passenger through use of an automatic door and ramp system. In addition, two regular passengers are provided seating comfort at a level exceeding that of any present U.S. taxi model.

Passenger doors are bi-fold automated "phone-booth" type. The doors are spring-loaded to open and are held closed by latches in the "C" posts. When either inside or outside handle is pulled, the door opens forward and outward. Opening speed is controlled by an orificed hydraulic system. To close, either the driver or passenger pushes an electrical switch valving high-pressure water to a cylinder opposing the spring and closing the door. The trailing edges of the passenger doors are equipped with "sensitive edge" switches to reverse the door motion upon encountering an obstacle.

The doors, being located in close proximity to seated passengers, are required to meet latch retention and side door strength criteria as set forth in the Federal Motor Vehicle Safety Standards (FMVSS) 206 and 214. The 38 in. (97 cm.) wide door opening and center hinge configuration ruled out the normal approach of employing a structural horizontal beam between rigid pillars. Instead, a waist-high hinge is added to the "B" pillar, attached to a tubular tension member joined to the door latch pin. This tension member is itself hinged at the door center. Closing and latching the door completes a

structurally sound tension member from "B" pillar to "C" pillar.

The requirement for automatic unassisted loading and unloading of a wheelchair-seated passenger from a 5 in.-9 in. (13 cm.-23 cm.) curb height posed the major passenger-related design problem. The solution incorporates a ramp, 30 in. x 60 in. (76 cm. x 152 cm.), carried under the floor and deployed electrically out the right side of the vehicle.

The under-floor ramp location and chassis base structure result in a nominal floor height of 12.5 in. (32 cm.) above ground level. This was considered uncomfortably high for the aged and infirm, so a separate step is deployed automatically on the right side during door operation, providing an intermediate step height of 7.5 in. (19 cm.). This step rides on a parallelogram linkage and is directly linked to the door actuator.

Driver Requirements

Particular emphasis has been placed on driver-related aids. Accommodations include a tilting seatback adjustment, armrests, minimized control force levels, and a bullet-resistant security barrier between driver and passenger compartment. In the SPS design, the driver's seating position is 6 in. (15 cm.) to the left of the vehicle centerline and high enough to place the driver's eye location above the roof height of conventional vehicles. These provisions and the nearly continuous perimeter of deep window area afford the driver an excellent degree of vision.

*Three drawings of
SPS taxi prototype
showing front, rear,
and side views.*

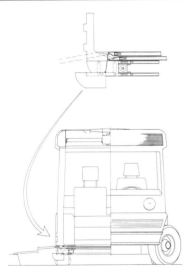

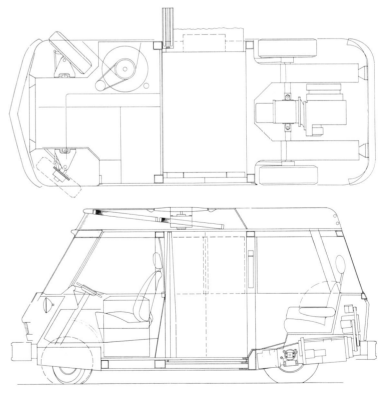

*Elevation and plan of
the SPS taxi prototype
with detail of the
sliding ramp.*

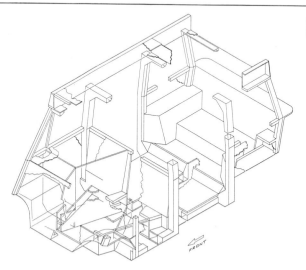

Unibody structure of SPS taxi prototype.

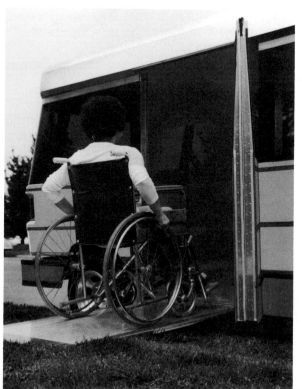

Side view of SPS prototype with wheelchair ramp extended.

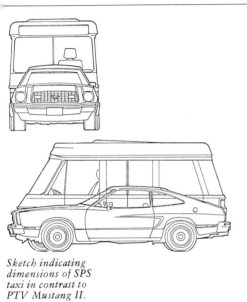

Sketch indicating dimensions of SPS taxi in contrast to PTV Mustang II.

Driver Security

Driver security requirements are met by providing a bullet-resistant partition between driver and passengers. The upper portion of the partition is ⅜ in. (0.95 cm.) thick GE Lexan MR4000. The criteria specified by DOT involve stopping a .45 caliber ACP bullet at point-blank range. Testing proved that weight could be saved over ballistic steel sheet by using .050 in. (1.3 mm.) thick 6AL-4V titanium alloy, which is incorporated in the sandwich panel forming the lower portion of the partition, and also in the driver's seat back.

Crash Safety Features

The bumper system is designed to meet the present requirements of FMVSS 215 and utilizes hollow trapezoidal blocks of bonded rubber and plastic which absorb impact energy through elastic deformation. The bumpers are designed to withstand impacts between 12 in. (30 cm.) and 20 in. (51 cm.) above ground level.

A number of safety systems are incorporated into the vehicle and steam power plant. The ignition system incorporates electronic startup sequencing and flame sensors. If an improper ignition or flameout occurs, the fuel supply is shut off automatically and the combustor and exhaust systems are purged of fuel vapors before a restart can be attempted. This system is similar to gas turbine technology.

All potentially hazardous steam lines are routed to minimize the possibility of rapid release of steam or hot water, either inside or outside the vehicle. The 850° F (454° C) high-pressure steam line to the expander passes through one of the primary horizontal beams in the chassis floor. The 220° F (104° C) low-pressure exhaust steam line to the condenser passes through the right-side "C" pillar and is surrounded by pour-in-place polyurethane foam insulation, which also serves to protect the tube.

Body Design and Special Features

The single most important factor in increasing overall vehicle efficiency is weight. The emphasis placed on minimizing total weight has been the overriding factor in many of the design tradeoffs involved, and is perhaps most evident in the design of the unibody structure.

After initial design work on the SPS taxi prototype, it was apparent that the conventional forms of mass-produced chassis/body construction were too heavy and too costly for use on a single prototype. These include ladder, X, and rail-type frames with separate non-structural bodies, and steel unit construction utilizing stamped sheet structure with add-on subframes to carry high point loads.

Multi-tubular "space-frame" construction was eliminated because of the need for a flat, low floor and the difficulty involved in triangulating the vertical panels while retaining visibility.

The basic SPS taxi box-shape with low floor and tall sides lends itself naturally to unit or monoque construction and takes advantage of the large cross-sectional area of the total vehicle to obtain excellent overall torsional rigidity and bending strength. Material selection was less obvious. Fiberglass reinforced plastic would require either expensive sandwich-construction techniques or excessive material thickness to reduce panel drumming. The construction technique uses a semi-monocoque skin consisting of separate bonded aluminum honeycomb sandwich panels bolted or bonded to a base frame structure.

The base frame structure serves as alignment jig for the skin panels, as attachment points for doors, ramp, and suspension subframes, and as a load path for the major crash forces. The elements of the beam structure are .062 in. (1.6 mm.) thick 5052-H34 aluminum sheet, brake-formed and closed by blind rivets. These box beams are then joined by TIG welding. Flanged access and lightening holes are provided in the major cross beams. No elaborate fixturing was found necessary during fabrication, but a flat surface table was used. Total weight of the welded base structure, including the exhaust steam line in the right-side "C" pillar, foam-in place polyurethane foam insulation, and passenger door locks and latches is 92 lbs. (42 kg.).

To the base structure are attached the stressed panels forming the semi-monocoque chassis. Exterior panels and those required for access are bolted in place, and all others are permanently bonded in place. Each panel consists of a core

of hexcell aluminum foil honeycomb, 5052 alloy, of .001 in. (.03 mm.) thickness, and two skins of .012 in.–.040 in. (.3 mm.–1.0 mm.) thick 7075-T6 aluminum, bonded under heat and pressure with an epoxy adhesive. Core thickness varies from .375 in.–1.50 in. (9.5 mm.–38 mm.). Open cells in exposed edges are filled with a mixture of structural epoxy adhesive and a low-density filler, and mating edges are bonded in place using .040 in. (1 mm.) thick aluminum doublers.

The bonded monocoque chassis structure possesses attractive stiffness-to-weight ratios in torsion and bending, but care must be taken to spread external loads adequately to avoid local panel failure. Separate welded tubular subframes are therefore attached to both front and rear to carry suspension components. These subframes are constructed of .049 in.–.062 in. (1.3 mm.–1.6 mm.) wall mild steel tubing and sheet, TIG welded, using fixtures to locate critical points.

The complete chassis structure weight is 396 lbs. (180 kg.). The DuPont Lucite AR windows contribute materially to overall chassis rigidity.

Material thickness selection for nearly all structural chassis members was computer calculated by three iterations of the NASTRAN finite element stress analysis program. This method was also used to establish compliance with several of the Federal Motor Vehicle Safety Standards for passenger vehicles, notably FMVSS 215 and 216 for exterior protection and roof crush resistance. Computer results indicate an axle-to-axle torsional stiffness of 21,000 lb.-ft. per degree (2900 kg.-meters per degree), approximately four times that of a standard sedan.

A Chrysler front torsion bar system has been adapted to all four wheels, with provision for quick ride height adjustment at each lower suspension arm. Maintaining desired ride height with changing load is achieved by the use of self-leveling shock absorbers, which convert suspension motion into internal pressurization to maintain length.

All suspension components are fabricated from high-strength steel alloys for light weight. Provision has been made for fine tuning of both front and rear suspension systems during development testing.

The steering system presents an interesting challenge and a novel solution. The design turning-circle goal of 32 ft. (9.8 m) translates to an outer wheel steering angle of approximately 45°, compared to 32°–35° on conventional vehicles. To avoid the power loss and weight penalty of a power-boosted steering system, a lightweight rack-and-pinion is used which incorporates a spur gear reduction between the steering column input shaft and the pinion gear. This gearset achieves a numerically higher steering ratio and permits changes in ratio during testing.

A primary consideration for the braking system was the avoidance of a power-boost system. At the front, a lightweight caliper and disc are used, and the rear is a lightened Corvair drum system. Separate pressure switches and fluid reservoirs are included to comply with Federal standards.

Performance goals for the SPS taxi prototype include a top speed of 60 mph (97 km./hr.), fuel consumption of 12 mpg (5.1 km./liter) over the LA4 driving cycle emissions test, and fuel capacity of 10 gallons (38 liters)—sufficient to last through an 8-hour shift in use as an urban taxi.

Consumption and Pollution
The SPS taxi prototype has placed great emphasis on the current and anticipated petroleum shortage, and urban air pollution. The requirements for low pollutant emissions and alternate fuel capabilities are met by an improved version of the External Combustion Engine (ECE) system developed by SPS under the 1974 California Clean Car Project. This system has been operated on several alternate fuels, including kerosene, diesel fuel, methanol, and distillate coal oil.

Propulsion and Engine
Current vehicular ECE systems are at a disadvantage in terms of power system weight. It is therefore essential to reduce total power requirement in three areas: vehicle and power system parasitic accessory loads, power transmission losses, and road resistance.

The power system itself is a further development of the system produced for the 1974 California Clean Car Project. It uses a 4-cylinder, compound expansion, double acting variable cutoff expander, monotube flash boiler, 2-speed automatic transaxle without torque converter, and fixed-core aluminum tube-and-fin condenser. Parasitic power loss has been reduced in comparison with the Cal-Car system in several areas, notably increased expander and feedwater pump efficiency, a roof-mounted condenser of increased core area and reduced fan power, and increased combustor and combustion air fan efficiency. Radial ply tires are used to minimize rolling resistance.

Aerodynamic drag is minimized by the use of a V-shaped nose in plan view, smoothly rounded front corners, and virtually flush external skin and window surfaces.
—Steam Power Systems

References

Burtz, R. D.; Schneider, P. H.; Burton, R. L.; Younger, F. C.; and Duffy, T. E. Paper 749128, "Design and Performance of a Baseline Rankine Cycle Automobile." Proceedings of the 9th Intersociety Energy Conversion Engineering Conference, 1974.

Hauck, R. W.; Wenstrom, M.; and Renner, R. A. "The California Clean Car Project—Final Report." Assembly Office of Research, California Legislature, Sacramento, Cal., January, 1975.

Renner, R. A., "Experience with Steam Cars in California." Paper 750069 presented at SAE Automotive Engineering Congress and Exposition, Detroit, Mich., February, 1975.

Schneider, P. H., "Steam Power Systems' California Clean Air Project." Paper 750070 presented at SAE Automotive Engineering Congress and Exposition, Detroit, Mich., February, 1975.

U.S. Department of Transportation, Urban Mass Transportation Administration, Contract No. DOT-UT-50019, Project No. CA-06-0079.

Volvo Taxi Prototype

Manufacturer	A. B. Volvo, Göteborg, Sweden
Engine	6-cylinder diesel, in line, swirl chamber type 146 cu. in. 2400 cu. cm. 70 hp SAE at 4500 rpm
Performance Max. speed Acceleration Fuel consumption Fuel type Emission	 85 mph 136 km./h 0 to 60 mph in 19.5 seconds 22 to 24 mpg Diesel fuel Meets all present and proposed Federal emission requirements. HC–0.7, CO–3.4, NOX–2.0 g/mile
Body frame	Unitized body
Transmission	3-speed automatic
Drive	Front-wheel drive
Steering Type Turn radius	 Rack and pinion, power-assisted 17 ft. 5.2 m.
Braking system front & rear	 Triangular split system. Servo emergency brake on rear wheels operating on drums
Suspension front/rear	 Wishbones and combined steel and urethane springs/De Dion axle trailing links and rod, combined steel and urethane springs
Overall dimensions Max. length Max. width Max. height Wheelbase	 172.5 in. 438 cm. 75.6 in. 192 cm. 67.7 in. 172 cm. 120 in. 300 cm.
Track front/rear	60 in./ 150 cm./ 63 in. 160 cm.
Interior dimensions passenger compartment Length Width Headroom over aisle	 63 in. 160 cm. 63 in. 160 cm. 54.3 in. 138 cm.

Weight	3740 lb.	1700 kg.
Ground clearance	7 in.	18 cm.
Entry height	11.8 in.	30 cm.
General data	Carries 3 to 4 passengers plus driver, space for wheelchair; passenger sliding door; air-conditioned. By extending the wheelbase 31.5 in. (80 cm.) it can be used as an ambulance, large jitney taxi, etc. Taximeter of electronic type with separate display in passenger compartment.	

Volvo

The purpose of Volvo's participation in the Taxi Project is to develop a taxicab specifically designed for today's environment. The Volvo experimental taxi is not to be seen as a prototype ready for production, but as a conception, a basis for future development in taxi services.

In Volvo's opinion, the transport problems of our society cannot be solved by products resulting from a utopian ideal; we believe in simple and practical solutions.

As long ago as 1972, at the UN's Environmental Conference in Stockholm, Volvo took on the full responsibility of a motor vehicle manufacturer, with particular emphasis on solving urban traffic problems. The solution to these problems is not to be found in a war against the motor car, but in a comprehensive understanding of the car's benefits.

With these aims, it is understandable that Volvo is interested in the possibilities offered by a well-organized and correctly utilized taxi system. Society's demands on urban transportation will steadily grow, not only in the form of an increasing volume of traffic, but also in the qualitative and functional aspects of an individual's mobility in the total structure of urban transportation.

The taxi has a considerably larger potential in a public transport system than is manifest at present. However, a broadening of its scope requires a parallel development of the taxi's purely engineering aspects and of the operating techniques which must form the basis for the vehicle's efficient and worthwhile use.

Vehicular safety, versatility, and diversification of action have been the cornerstones of the Volvo concept. The experimental taxi now presented by Volvo is, as far as passenger safety is concerned, based on the Company's many years of experience. Special emphasis has been placed on combining these safety aspects with comfort for both driver and passengers. The vehicle is presented as one ideally adapted to the heavy and aggressive traffic of today's cities.

Another of Volvo's considerations was to offer the disabled and infirm a safer and more comfortable transport alternative than that offered by today's cabs. In the Volvo experimental taxi it is much easier for the disabled to enter and leave the vehicle, even when sitting in a wheelchair.

The Volvo Taxi

The Volvo taxi is spacious, yet compact. The overall length is 172.4 in. (437 cm.), which is approximately a foot and a half shorter than the taxis commonly used in New York today.

The wheelbase is 118.2 in. (300 cm.). Overall width is 74.8 in. (190 cm.), height 67.7 in. (172 cm.), curb-weight approximately 3300 lb. (1500 kg.), and gross weight 4400 lb. (2000 kg.).

The car has front-wheel drive and a configuration which gives an ideal fifty-fifty distribution of weight in all situations.

The Volvo taxi has very short front and rear overhangs, which mean good vision and a tight turning circle. Despite the front-wheel drive, the full lock angle on the inner wheel is not less than 44° and the turning-circle diameter is only about 34 ft. (10.4 m.).

The body is built according to the Volvo "safety cage principle"; heavy closed profile members surround the entire occupant area, while the front and rear sections are energy-absorbing crumple zones. The doors and flanks of the vehicle incorporate built-in protection in the form of tubular steel members, and the floor is reinforced by five cross members.

The engine is mounted forward of the driver—a position which gives the best protection in the event of a crash.

Both the front and rear bumper are impact-absorbing and comply with the 5 mph crash impact requirement by a wide margin. Along the flanks of the vehicle runs a heavy-duty rubber molding at a strategic height—chosen to reduce the extent of the often slight yet expensive damage which is so usual in city traffic.

In the roof are two condenser fans for the air conditioning system. The trailing lip of the roofline is shaped knifelike for better aerodynamic efficiency and to reduce the swirling up of road dirt onto the rear window.

Passengers

The passengers will experience the Volvo taxi as being convenient and comfortable. The right-hand door is an electrically operated sliding door which is controlled by the driver. The door slides forward to open. The advantages are that the door aperture is extra wide for ease of entry and exit and the door does not block the sidewalk.

Entry height is not much higher than the sidewalk itself, only 11.8 in. (30 cm.) above ground level.

The ground clearance of the taxi is 7 in. (18 cm.), which is more than sufficient for operation on bad surfaces.

The floor is slightly convex, and there are no doorsills, so that the interior is easy to clean.

The passengers sit separate from the driver. The rear seat is intended for two,

Drawing, from the
left side, indicating
dimensions.

Plan indicating
dimensions.

67.7

7.1

118.1
172.4

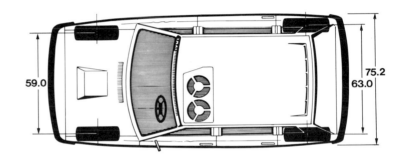

59.0

75.2
63.0

ngine and drive
aft.

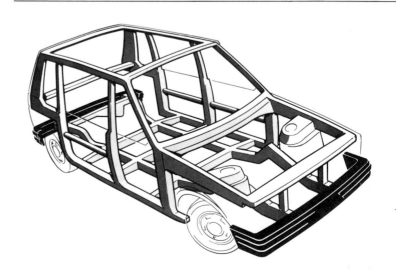

Safety-cage construc-
tion of the body
frame.

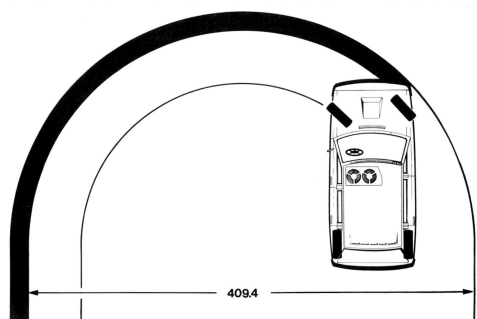

409.4

Drawing indicating
the turning circle.

Volvo taxi seen from
the right side, with
large sliding door.

Driver's seat.

and there is a center armrest. This can be folded to make room for three passengers. Comfort is assured by the anatomically correct seat design, plus high sitting height and generous legroom.

Instead of seat belts, Volvo has developed a safety bar to prevent passengers from being thrown forward during emergency braking or in a crash. The bar is anchored to the vehicle's body just above waist height and folds up against the roof when not in use. To use the safety bar, the passenger pulls it down. In its lowered position, the bar can be adjusted to suit the height of the passengers. Thus it provides excellent protection from both front and sides and is also, because of its soft padding, a convenient armrest.

Volvo chose this type of safety restraint for its taxi since experience has shown that taxi passengers are very reluctant to use the conventional type of seat belt.

The Volvo taxi features a full heating and ventilation system incorporating air conditioning. It is also fitted with a stereo radio with twin speakers. The rear side windows are electrically operated.

On the right, ahead of the rear seat, is room for luggage. This space can also be used for an extra passenger since it is equipped with a folding, rear-facing seat.

Driver Requirements
The driving area in the Volvo taxi is specifically designed for long, arduous working shifts in the worst of city traffic.

The driving seat incorporates a wide range of adjustments. Furthermore, the backrest is fully adjustable and incorporates a lumbar support. Whatever his build, the driver can sit comfortably and is always ensured good vision.

The driving seat has a built-in head restraint and is unusual in design since it is asymmetrical in shape. The right-hand side incorporates extra padding toward the front and sides of both the cushion and backrest to give better lateral support. The left-hand side of the cushion is rounded to facilitate the driver's entry and exit. Lateral support from the left is provided by the closed door. The driving seat is also equipped with a three-point inertia reel seat belt.

Controls of a similar nature are fitted in groups. For example, all lighting controls are on the left-hand side of the wheel, wipers-washers on the right, and so on.

In addition, the controls are designed to minimize the risk of inadvertent use. Pull controls have one particular shape, twist controls another, and flip controls a third.

All controls which are specific to a taxi—for example, the taximeter—have been mounted separate from the others, since they are not used while the vehicle is actually moving. The taxi controls, however, are still within easy arm's reach.

1 The dashboard instruments are deeply recessed for the following two reasons:

a) There is less risk of distracting reflections.

b) Transition from close-up viewing (instruments) to long-distance viewing (surrounding traffic) will not be disturbing to the driver's eyes.

2 The steering wheel has a built-in crumple zone which yields in a collision.

3 The taxi has a three-stage automatic transmission which incorporates an acoustic backing-up warner.

4 The windshield is extra large, considerably larger than existing requirements demand.

5 The heating and ventilation—air conditioning system is of an air-blending type and reacts considerably faster than a system with a conventional water-valve control system. A single lever permits the driver to set the required temperature, which the system then maintains automatically.

6 Other features of the driving area include a writing table with reading lamp, a safe box, and a small refrigerator for drinks.

7 All of the doors are coupled to a system permitting them to be locked centrally by the driver. A warning light shows the driver if any of the doors is not completely locked. The driver's door has an opening angle of not less than 80°, and a red light warns oncoming traffic when it is open. This also applies to the passenger door on the left-hand side.

Side bumper.

Dashboard.

Condenser fans and roof line.

Front bumper.

Indication of:
A) grab handle,
B) air-conditioning oulet, C) volume control for stereo radio.

Rear seat, armrest down, safety bar in roof.

Height adjustment knob of the safety bar.

Rear seat accommodating passenger with the safety bar in use.

...terior seen from ...ight side, rear seat ...lded.

Luggage space in pas-
senger compartment.
Extra seat folded
when not in use.

Extra seat, in position
for use.

Control for electri-
cally powered
window, also showing
lighter and ashtray.

Engine

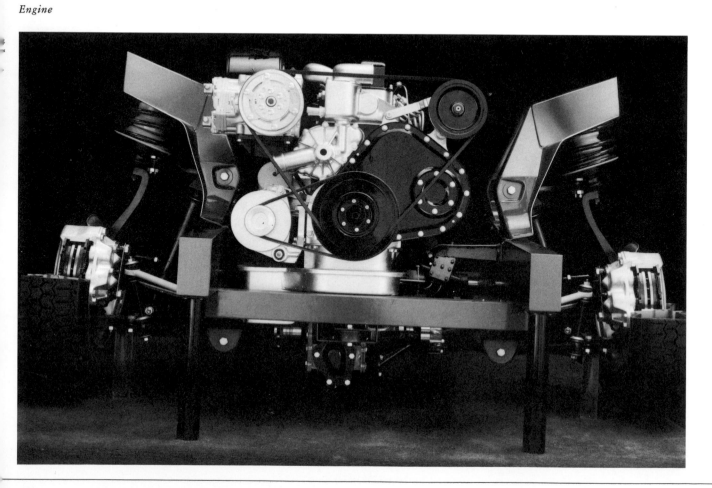

The driver is separated from the passengers by a partition consisting of bulletproof glass and armored steel. The entire partition, including the speaking box and payment box, is bulletproof.

Engine
The engine is an in-line, 6-cylinder, swirl combustion chamber diesel of 70 h.p. at 4500 rpm. It is prepared for turbo supercharging, which gives an output increase of between 15 and 20 h.p. The engine conforms with the existing exhaust emission requirements by a good margin.

The Volvo taxi has a maximum speed of better than 75 mph (120 kmph) and acceleration capabilities which give it ample performance for city traffic.

Body Design and Special Features
Transmission
On the rear of the automatic gearbox is a drop gear with chain transmission which drives a forward-pointing propshaft. Thanks to this layout, the engine and final drive are entirely separate, giving the Volvo taxi a very quiet and smooth transmission.

Hydraulics
The Volvo taxi is equipped with a high-pressure (150 bar.) central hydraulic system for brakes and steering. This means extra safety and long service life.

Electrical Center
The fuseboxes, including automatically resetting fuses, are mounted behind the driving seat. The space to the right of the driver is occupied by the power

supply, heating–ventilation–air conditioning system, etc.

Invalid Taxi
The low floor and the high, straight-backed sitting posture are ideal for the infirm or disabled.

Folding up the right-hand section of the rear seat provides space for a wheelchair passenger—with room for the accompanying passenger on the left side of the seat. There is no difficulty in getting a wheelchair into the Volvo taxi from normal sidewalk heights.

Development Possibilities
The Volvo taxi is intended for a maximum of 3+1 occupants and luggage; but, if the wheelbase is extended 31 in. (80 cm.), the taxi can easily be built as a mini-bus, with three seat rows for nine passengers. This opens up a wealth of other possibilities: the Volvo taxi design can also be used for an ambulance, a large station wagon, van—practically any type of special vehicle.

All basic systems in the prototype are dimensioned for the maximum vehicle length, this applying to all items of a safety nature.

Invalid Transport Service
The fact that the Volvo taxi is also an ideal vehicle for transporting invalids implies a considerable potential for the vehicle and thereby makes it attractive economically: for example, during periods of the day when the demand for normal taxi service is relatively low, the Volvo taxi can serve as a means of

Large windshield.

Writing table with
lamp.

Left side doors show-
ing warning lights.

Central locking device with warning light.

Ventilation controls.

Safe deposit box.

Seen on the sliding driver-passenger window partition are: A) loudspeaker, B) air-conditioning unit, C) unit for communication, D) volume control for loudspeaker, E) payment box, F) air vents.

Refrigerator for drinks.

Luggage compartment.

Drawing (interior)
of mini-bus with
passengers.

*Adaptation of Volvo
taxi as an ambulance.*

149.6

*Wheelchair moving
into the compartment
from the sidewalk.*

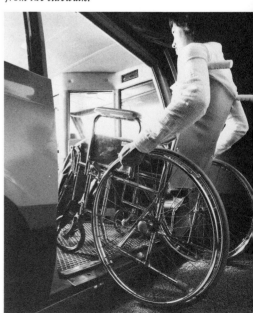

*Drawing of Volvo
taxi, adaptation as
station wagon.*

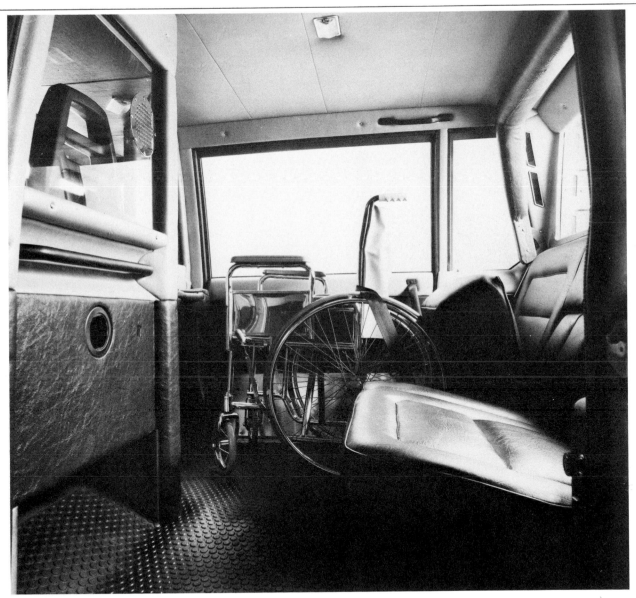

Forward-facing seat tilted up to accommodate wheelchair.

transportation for organizations for the physically handicapped or, as in Sweden, the social authorities.
In Gothenburg, for example, which is Sweden's second largest city, with a population of 500,000, no less than 1.2 million Invalid Transport Service journeys are made annually—and of these 90 per cent are carried out by taxis.

Volvo Tele-bus
The Volvo taxi, and particularly the extended mini-bus version, is the ideal vehicle for a demand-response system in which a smaller bus is sufficient to satisfy passenger volumes in an economical manner.

Volvo has developed one of these demand-response systems, and at present it is being tested in the town of Boras in Sweden. This system is based on a main route where taxis are dispatched every half-hour if orders have been incoming. Branch-off runs are made from this route when a passenger has telephoned previously and ordered the bus to any of the bus stops off the main route.

For the passengers this system means that they can order the bus to pick them up at their bus stop by dialing the tele-bus number and then dialing the number of their bus stop. All of the information needed by the passenger to order a bus journey correctly is given by an answering system. The system is entirely automatic, and the only personnel requirements are drivers.

The equipment consists of:

1 receiver for in-dialing messages
2 answering machine for instructions and confirmation
3 storage for incoming orders
4 printer for running schedule
5 control logic

At departure, the driver presses a button and is given a list of the bus stops where customers are waiting to be picked up. This system can also be used for commuting lines to a terminal from which larger units can run.

The tele-bus system means that bus traffic can offer excellent service at a lower cost than is normally required:

1 The distance which the bus travels from terminus to terminus can vary.

2 Empty running is minimized, since the driver knows in advance which bus stops he is to drive to.

This is one type of tele-bus system. The same equipment can be used for other types of demand-response system to suit the needs and capacities of the area in question.
—Volvo

Volkswagen Taxi Prototype

Manufacturer	Volkswagenwerk, Wolfsburg, West Germany
Engine	Hybrid power plant (a combination of gasoline- and electric-powered engine) Gasoline engine: 50 DIN hp 1600 cu. cm. Electric engine: Bosch GmbH; DC shunt motor, 130 v/16 kw continuous duty, 32 kw short duty
Performance	
Max. speed	43.5 mph 70 km./h in electric mode 64.6 mph 104 km./h in hybrid power mode
Acceleration	0 to 62 mph in 31 seconds
Fuel consumption	20 mpg 8.5 km/l.
Fuel type	Gasoline
Emission	Electric operation: no exhaust Hybrid power operation: meets current Federal emission requirements
Body frame	Unitized body
Transmission	Torque converter coupled through an automatic clutch
Drive	Rear-wheel drive (rear engine)
Steering	
Type	Worm and roller
Turn radius	18.5 ft. 5.65 m.
Braking system	
front/rear	Disc/drum
Suspension	
front/rear	Independent trailing arms/semi-trailing arm
Overall dimensions	
Max. length	179 in. 454 cm.
Max. width	69.3 in. 176 cm.
Max. height	77 in. 195.5 cm.
Wheelbase	94.5 in. 240 cm.
Track front/rear	54.9 in./ 139.5 cm./ 57.3 in. 145.5 cm.
Interior dimensions	
passenger compartment	
Length	50 in. 127 cm.
Width	61.8 in. 157 cm.
Headroom over aisle	54.2 in. 137.5 cm.

Weight	4740 lb. 2133 kg.
Ground clearance	7.1 in. 18 cm.
Entry height	19.5 in. 49.5 cm.
General data	Carries 4 to 5 passengers plus driver; space for wheelchair; retractable step; sliding door; air-conditioned

Volkswagen

A taxi for traffic of the future must meet a number of requirements that are not met by the taxis of today.

At present taxis differ primarily from regular sedans only as regards color. The 40 sq. ft. of interior space provided by today's average taxi compares with some 100 sq. ft. of space that the vehicle requires on the street. Today's taxis do not permit passengers to exit with opened umbrellas, nor to move baby carriages into the vehicles. They are too wide and too low; their fuel consumption and exhaust emissions are too high. Today's taxis have not been built for their special purpose.

The Museum of Modern Art has established the following criteria for a taxi of the future:

1 It must provide safety, comfort and an extreme degree of maneuverability.

2 Passengers must be able to enter and leave the vehicle easily and be accommodated comfortably once inside.

3 The vehicle must be compact and offer a highly favorable ratio between overall length and payload space.

4 The vehicle must offer excellent driveability and provide above-average driving comfort.

5 It must be extremely economical and must produce a minimum of adverse effects on the environment.

These requirements can scarcely be met by a vehicle of conventional design. Accordingly, a concept must be developed to make a vehicle meet the requirements. This concept has already been realized in many respects in the Volkswagen Transporter which is the basis for the VW Station Wagon, usually referred to as the Volkswagen Micro-bus.

More than four million of these VW Transporter vehicles are in regular use throughout the world. The basic vehicle has demonstrated its outstanding qualities over countless miles under varying conditions. It is economical, sturdy, and uniquely comfortable and spacious.

Passengers:
Accommodations
The passengers are accommodated on four single seats. Three of them face the front, and can be adjusted individually for full seating comfort. The fourth seat faces the rear. Passenger legroom is considerably greater than in conventional sedans. Interior dimensions permit easy accommodation of either a baby carriage or a wheelchair.

Luggage
The passenger can carry hand luggage with him as he enters the vehicle. To secure luggage during a taxi trip, a restraining device can be folded down from the wall which separates the passengers from the driver's compartment. The passenger compartment allows plenty of room for hand luggage without inconveniencing the occupants. In addition, a separate rear compartment with a capacity of about 35 cu. ft. accommodates large pieces of luggage or other cargo. This rear compartment is accessible both from inside and outside the vehicle, the latter through a tailgate whose lock is controlled from the driver's seat. The passenger can load and unload luggage himself.

Seating, Support and Restraints
The anatomically designed passenger seats are intended for single occupancy. They are equipped with folding armrests, integrated head-restraints, and adjustable seatbacks. The seat covers were chosen for ventilation, durability, and a texture to prevent slipping. Each seat is equipped with a lap-type seat belt.

Passenger-Driver Separation
For a number of reasons, a wall has been erected to separate driver and passenger. To facilitate communication, the VW taxi is equipped with an intercom unit. A large window in the dividing wall permits visual contact between the driver and passengers and enables the latter to view the taxi meter. Fares may be passed from passenger to driver through a transfer device in the dividing wall.

Comfort and Convenience
The vehicle's interior has been decorated with dense, noise-insulating materials, and an air conditioning system assures cool temperatures during peak summer heat. The Volkswagen taxi also is equipped with a gasoline-powered auxiliary heating system for midwinter when the vehicle is parked with its engine shut down.

Dimensions
Floor area of the passenger compartment measures 61.75 in. (157 cm.) across and a maximum of 50 in. (127 cm.) from front to rear. Maximum height from floor to headliner is 54.25 in. (138 cm.)

Hiproom measured at the forward-facing passenger seats is 60.6 in. (154 cm.), shoulder room is 59.25 in. (150.5 cm.), headroom is 40.25 in. (102 cm.), and legroom, measured from the rear of the seat bottoms to the base of the security wall, is 70.25 in. (178.5 cm.). Each body-contoured seat is 18 in. (45 cm.) wide.

Indication of V W prototype's interior space with accommodation for four passengers.

The bulletproof glass window in the security wall is 48.25 in. (123 cm.) wide at the lower edge and 10.4 in. (26 cm.) high.

Accessibility

Large sliding doors, 41.75 in. (106 cm.) wide and 48.25 in. high (122.5 cm.) on both right and left of the VW taxi permit easy entrance. They also constitute an important safety element, as they enable passengers to enter and leave the vehicle at either right or left curb-side. The right-hand door, which will obviously have the greater use, has an electric remote control so that it may be opened and closed by the driver. A running board automatically extends from the vehicle when the right door opens to assist passengers when entering or leaving the taxi. The sliding doors do not obstruct traffic flow as is the case with conventionally hinged swing-out doors.

Driver Requirements: General

The vehicle is equipped with a semi-trailing arm rear axle; front independent suspension with trailing arms and stabilizers; worm-gear steering and hydraulic steering damper; dual-circuit brake system with front disc and rear drum brakes; deceleration-dependent brake force regulator; brake power booster; and steel-belted radial tires. The VW taxi has the same sort of suspension normally found in sports cars.

Security

A bulletproof wall, with bulletproof window, gives the driver special anti-crime protection.

Comfort, Convenience, and Crash Safety

Taxi drivers are required to spend prolonged periods behind the wheel. They must adjust their thinking to fast-changing street conditions and make quick decisions in critical traffic situations. A vehicle designed to counteract driver fatigue constitutes an important contribution to taxi safety. Good suspension comfort is provided by long spring travel and low spring rates on both the front and rear axle in conjunction with carefully tuned damping. The driver's seat is equipped with a three-point retractable safety belt system. The vehicle's operating controls were designed in accordance with the latest ergonomic findings. The type of automatic transmission employed is a major factor in terms of driver convenience and relief from fatigue.

Dimensions

The driver's bucket-type seat is 20.25 in. (51 cm.) wide, the seat-back rising 30.25 in. (77 cm.) above the cushion.

Driver hiproom is 33 in. (84 cm.), shoulder room 58.25 in. (148 cm.), headroom 38.5 in. (98 cm.) and legroom, measured from the rear of the seat cushion to the heel point of the accelerator pedal, is 40.25 in. (102 cm.).

A glovebox built into the right of the vehicle's dashboard measures 17 in. (43 cm.) wide, is 6 in. (15 cm.) high and 9 in. (23 cm.) deep.

Access to the driver's compartment is through the left front door, which is 42.25 in. (107 cm.) at its widest dimension and 50 in. (127 cm.) at its maximum height.

A large window in the VW dividing wall permits visual contact between the passengers and the driver. Fares may be passed through a small sliding tray in the partition.

Large sliding doors permit easy entrance and exit from the taxi.

Luggage accommodation in the VW prototype.

Interior dimensions permit easy accommodation of either a baby carriage or a wheelchair.

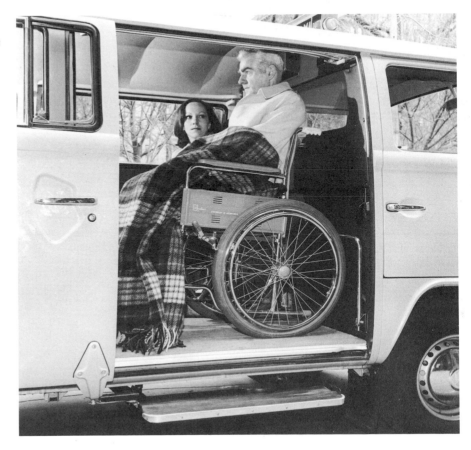

Driver Vision

The Volkswagen has been designed to provide excellent driver visibility under varied conditions, including exit from blind driveways and passage through congested intersections. Because the vehicle has no front hood and the driver's seat is relatively high above street level, the operator has a good view of his environment. This increased visibility also eliminates much of the tedium drivers face in heavy traffic.

Vehicle Identification

The VW taxi fulfills the requirements for vehicle color and an easily visible taxi light mounted on the roof.

Crash Safety Features

Experts in forensic medicine have recognized that many injuries in both passenger cars and trucks are caused by the steering wheel and steering column.

In their efforts to offer taxi drivers the same safety benefits offered by a standard car, Volkswagen has developed a special safety steering control system for the Transporter. This consists essentially of a collapsible support which connects the driver end of the steering wheel to the dashboard. This connection folds up at a preselected point to help absorb the impact in the event of the driver's striking the steering wheel during an accident. In case of frontal impact, the folding also limits steering wheel or dashboard intrusion into the driver compartment.

To minimize injuries, the VW Transporter is equipped with a padded dashboard; operating buttons, levers, and the

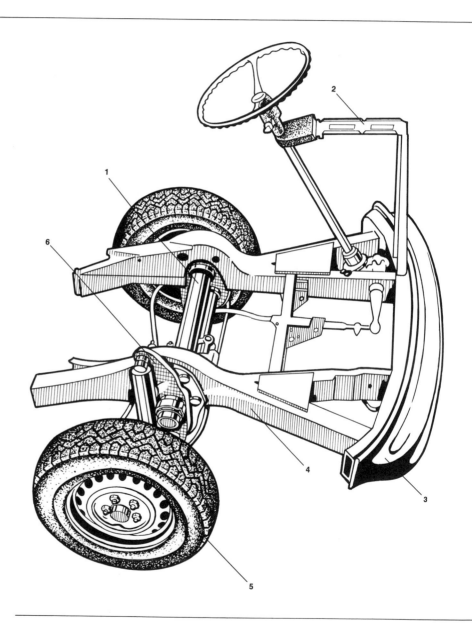

1 Tube-En-
  closed Tor-
  sion Bar
  Spring
2 Collapsible
  Steering-
  Column
  Support
3 Energy-
  Absorbing
  Bumper
  Reinforce-
  ment
4 Energy-Ab-
  sorbing
  Fork Frame
5 Steel-Belted
  Radial Tires
6 Independent
  Double
  Trailing Arm
  Suspension

vehicle's few protruding edges are also padded. The seat backs and head restraints meet all existing safety requirements.

Chassis Design Safety Features
Volkswagen, like other car manufacturers, is intensely concerned with safety research. A modern passenger vehicle should be so designed that it provides a high degree of protection for its occupants in event of collision. When the point is reached at which active safety measures are no longer sufficient to prevent accidents, passive safety measures are needed.

A deformation element immediately behind the vehicle's front bumper absorbs impact energy. Four stiff longitudinal beams behind the energy-absorbing element help prevent compression-type collapse of the driver cabin regardless of whether the vehicle undergoes frontal, diagonal, or corner impact.

Body Design and Special Features
The VW Transporter incorporates a number of standard features which are important to the taxi prototype. The vehicle has sliding side doors for safe entry and exit of its passengers. Its wide "picture windows" assure all-around visibility for both driver and passengers. Its rear engine and rear wheel drive permit a flat interior floor, as opposed to the driveshaft tunnel found in most vehicles.

In addition, the VW Transporter incorporates longitudinal door beams. By transmitting side impact forces throughout the vehicle's frame, the

beams help maintain the cabin configuration. Together with the vertical beams, they also protect the driver and front-seat passenger in the event of a lateral collision.

Because the VW taxi driver and passengers are positioned above the usual impact zone, lateral collisions pose substantially less threat to them than to occupants of conventional passenger cars.

In the case of a rear impact, the large sheet-metal surface is advantageous both to the impacting vehicle which collides with the metal and to the VW Transporter.

All door locks and hinges, including those of the sliding doors and the tailgate, are constructed in such a manner that they do not spring open during impact and vehicle roll-over tests.

Fuel Consumption and Air Pollution
Fuel consumption of the hybrid power plant developed for the VW taxi compares favorably with that of the regular VW Transporter's 2-liter fuel injection engine. VW's 1976-model Transporters with automatic transmissions and 2-liter engines received Environmental Protection Agency fuel economy ratings of 18 mph in simulated city traffic, 24 mph in highway operation, and a combined city/highway fuel economy rating of 20 mph.

Propulsion and Engine
Volkswagen has developed a hybrid power plant for the VW taxi. This power plant—a combination of an

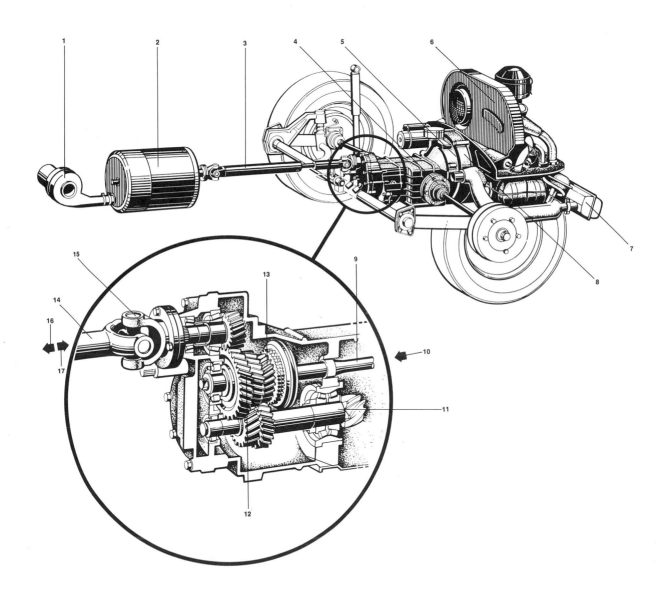

Hybrid Power Plant

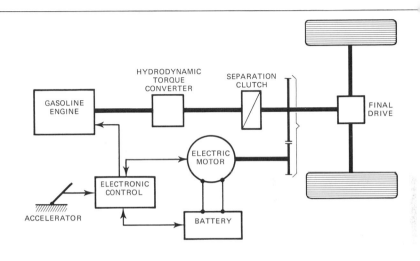

1 Cooling Fan
2 Electric
  Motor
3 Electric
  Motor Drive
  Shaft
4 Double-
  Jointed
  Rear Axle
5 Clutch
6 Air-Cooled
  Internal
  Combustion
  Engine
7 Muffler
8 Torque
  Converter
9 Engine
  Drive Shaft
10 Internal
  Combustion
  Engine
  Input

11 Hybrid
  Power to
  Rear Wheels
12 Forward
  Gearing
13 Reverse
  Gearing
14 Electric
  Motor Drive
  Shaft
15 Universal
  Joint
16 Input to
  Generator
  on Charge
  Mode
17 Output
  from Elec-
  tric Motor
  on Drive
  Mode

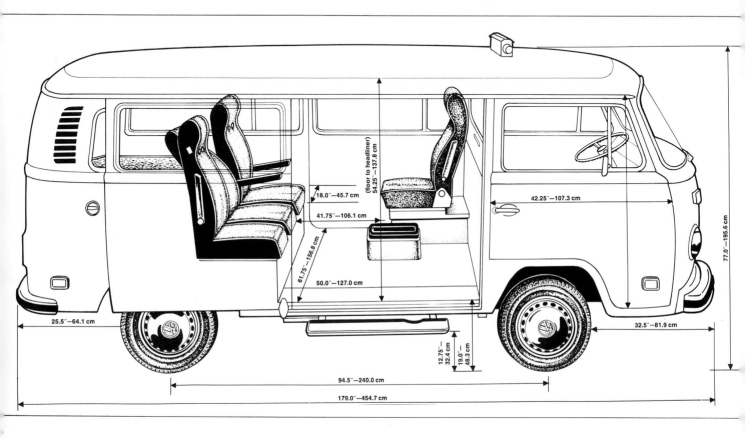

18.0″—45.7 cm

(floor to headliner)
54.25″—137.8 cm

41.75″—106.1 cm

42.25″—107.3 cm

61.75″—156.8 cm

50.0″—127.0 cm

77.0″—195.6 cm

25.5″—64.1 cm

32.5″—81.9 cm

12.75″—32.4 cm

19.0″—48.3 cm

94.5″—240.0 cm

179.0″—454.7 cm

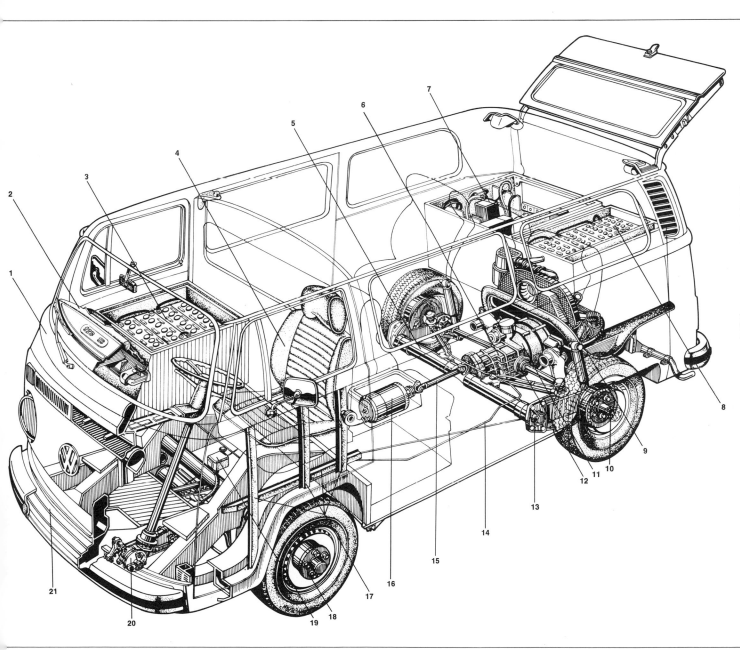

1 ...itized
...dy
...shboard
...dded
...orage
...tteries
... Electric
...ve Mode

4 Driver's
Body-Con-
toured Seat
with Head
Restraint
5 Tube-En-
closed Tor-
sion Bar
Spring

6 Trans-
mission
7 Electronic
Control Unit
8 Storage
Batteries for
Electric
Drive Mode

9 Air-Cooled
Internal
Combustion
Engine
10 Rear Drum
Brake
11 Double-
Jointed
Rear Axle

12 Independent
Trailing Arm
Suspension
13 Hydro-
dynamic
Torque
Converter
and Clutch

14 Hydraulic
Brake Lines
15 Electric
Motor Drive
Shaft

16 Electric
Motor
17 Door Rein-
forcement
Beams
18 Power-
Assisted
Disc Brake

19 Transparent
Brake-Fluid
Reservoir
20 Worm and
Roller
Steering
Gear Box
21 Deformation
Element

internal combustion engine and an electric motor—provides the advantages of both systems:

1   It produces no exhaust emissions when operated solely on the electric motor part of its power plant.

2   The only limit to the vehicle's operating range when running on hybrid operation is the capacity of its fuel tank. (Hybrid operation entails running the vehicle with the internal combustion engine and electric motor working in unison.) Overall operating range of the VW taxi thus is comparable to that of a conventional vehicle powered by an internal combustion engine.

The mode of operation of this power plant is explained by the following description of a standing-start acceleration process until desired speed has been reached:

After the gasoline engine has been started, the accelerator pedal governs the desired pulling power. The electric motor then develops a torque (a force that produces or tends to produce rotation or torsion) corresponding to this pulling power. This means that the electric motor carries the entire load in the beginning. At the same time, however, the gasoline engine develops a torque as its throttle valve is slowly opened. The torque of the electric motor can be decreased as the gasoline engine torque increases. This is done to save the battery, the decrease equaling the increase in the torque of the gasoline engine.

Indication of length and height of VW taxi in contrast to a typical American taxi.

VW Transporter shown in this crash-test photo was traveling at about 30 mph when it struck the immobile car ahead of it. Impact energy was absorbed so well by vehicle's front-end design that the Transporter was able to drive away from the test site under its own power.

Once the acceleration process has been completed, speed can be maintained either with the aid of the gasoline engine or with the electric motor alone, assuming that the individual motor output suffices to compensate for the vehicle driving resistance. If this is not the case, both motors are used simultaneously.

In the event that the gasoline engine produces more power than required, the excess is used to charge the battery while the vehicle is being driven. In this case, the electric motor serves as a generator.

As the photographs reveal, this hybrid power plant consists essentially of a gasoline engine with hydrodynamic torque converter and a separation clutch K as well as an electronically controlled electric motor E which is powered by a battery B. The electrical component E of the power plant is connected via the clutch to the output shaft of the hydrodynamic torque converter through a fixed ratio transmission.

The electronic control R controls the behavior of the individual power plant components and provides for smoother operation of the entire power plant depending on the driving state of the vehicle and the charge condition of the electrical energy storage unit. Part of this control is an electronic DC device to control electrical torque of the electric motor.

Because of this power plant system, the torque of the E motor is added to the converted torque of the gasoline engine. The momentary driving condition of the vehicle establishes the torque T_4 to be produced by the hybrid power plant and the speed of shaft number 4. Because of the coupling of the output shafts of the gasoline engine and the electric motor by the transmission I_{34}, both the output speed of the converter and the speed of the electric motor are determined. However, the torque contributions $T_E = T_3$ and $T_0 = T_1$ of the individual machines to the total torque T_4 are uncertain, where $T_4 = T_2 + T_3 \times I_{34}$. This makes it possible for the electric motor to smooth out rapid engine torque changes, either by adding to or absorbing any excess torque from the engine. This fact was taken into account when the control system was conceived.

The VW taxi can also be powered by the 2-liter air-cooled fuel injection engine used in the 1976 VW Transporter models marketed in the United States. This engine is similar in layout to those that have powered the VW Transporter over the years. In the Transporter (first built in 1950), engine, clutch, automatic transmission, and axle drive are combined into one compact unit for installation at the rear of the vehicle.

Specifications of the fuel injection
Transporter engine for 1976:

Mode of operation:	4-stroke gasoline engine
Bore:	3.7 in. (9.4 cm.)
Stroke:	2.8 in. (7.1 cm.)
Displacement:	1970 cc
Compression:	7.3
Output (SAE net):	67 h.p. at 4200 rpm
Max. Torque:	97 lb.-ft. at 3000 rpm

Emissions

When equipped with its hybrid power plant and operated solely on electric power, no noxious emissions are produced by the VW taxi.

Operated in the dual power mode, exhaust emissions are substantially lower than those from a conventional gasoline engine which meets current requirements of the Clean Air Act. This is because much of an internal combustion engine's emissions are due to rapid changes in throttle valve position, such as occur when the accelerator pedal is depressed or released quickly. The hybrid power plant is such that the electric motor carries the entire load at the start of the acceleration process, so the throttle valve can be opened slowly, producing relatively low emissions.

When operated in its third mode, totally gasoline-engine powered, the VW taxi has exhaust emission levels well within the limits of the Clean Air Act.

Cost and Maintenance

A tightly knit servicing organization in some 140 countries around the world is available for VW taxi operators. Both new and factory-rebuilt parts can be obtained from those facilities at reasonable prices.

Cost Reduction Requirements

Because the VW taxi uses a large number of off-the-shelf components, it does not require extensive retooling in manufacture.

—Volkswagen

Alfa Romeo Taxi Prototype

Manufacturer	Alfa Romeo, Milan, Italy		**Weight**	3520 lb.	1600 kg.
			Ground		
Engine	4-cycle, 4 cylinders in line, dual overhead cam 78 cu. in.　　　　1290 cu. cm. 60 hp SAE at 5600 rpm		**clearance** **Entry height** **General data**	6.3 in. 11.8 in. Carries 5 passengers plus driver; sliding door; retractable ramp for wheelchair; air-conditioned	16 cm. 30 cm.

Performance

Max. speed	75 mph	120 km./h
Acceleration	1 km. (0.6 mile) from standing, 50 seconds	
Fuel consumption	18 mpg	8.33 km./l.
Fuel type	Gasoline	
Emission	Meets present Federal standards	

Body frame　　Reinforced steel chassis with
roll-bar and supporting ribs

Transmission　4-speed

Drive　　　　Front-wheel drive

Steering

Type	Worm and roller	
Turn radius	17.3 ft.	5.25 m.

**Braking
system**

front/rear	Disc/drum

Suspension

front/rear	Independent with double tele- scopic hydraulic shock absorbers

**Overall
dimensions**

Max. length	162.6 in.	406.5 cm.
Max. width	69 in.	175 cm.
Max. height	70 in.	177 cm.
Wheelbase	90.5 in.	230 cm.
Track	56 in./	142 cm./
front/rear	58 in.	146 cm.

**Interior
dimensions**
passenger compartment

Length	75 in.	190 cm.
Width	55 in.	140 cm.
Headroom over aisle	55 in.	140 cm.

Alfa Romeo

Editor's Note: The Alfa Romeo prototype is being shown *hors concours*. Although this represents a model intended specifically for the European market, the Museum has decided to present it because Alfa Romeo has on its own chosen to construct it in accordance with the requirements laid down in the Design Specifications Manual prepared for the Taxi Project. The Museum was also interested in presenting it to the American public as an indication of the automobile industry's concern in the problems of urban transportation. The Alfa Romeo prototype is not proposed for manufacture in the United States, nor is it to be tested by the New York City Taxi and Limousine Commission.

Economic developments in recent years have focused attention on public transportation. In this field, the taxi occupies a unique position: it performs a public service for the community, and it accommodates private interests.

The intent of Alfa Romeo's design is to supply functional and practical solutions for the specific needs of driver, passengers, and traffic conditions, in addition to meeting conventional demands for efficiency and economy. Alfa Romeo commissioned Ital Design, under the creative direction of Giorgetto Giugiaro, to design a front-wheel-drive taxi based upon the prototype chassis of a small Alfa Romeo van and powered by Alfa Romeo's dual-overhead-cam 4-cylinder engine.

Behind this project stands the experience of Alfa Romeo in designing and producing motor vehicles known for their preventive safety concept and for their strength and durability developed on the racetrack—the ultimate proving ground.

Giorgetto Giugiaro has created a design prototype which provides spacious accommodations for passengers and luggage, exemplary comfort for all occupants, and new service features which are both useful and convenient under all operating conditions, even emergency situations.

Description of Prototype

The Alfa Romeo taxi prototype is constructed of mechanical parts already in production.

Chassis, engine, transmission, suspension, steering, and brakes have been taken directly from a small Alfa Romeo production van. This key decision makes possible generous accommodations for passengers and luggage. At the same time it provides a comfortable and protected driver's compartment due to the location of the engine directly over the front wheels. The elevated position of the driver's seat affords a point of visibility about 14 in. (35 cm.) above that in standard taxis.

Upon this van chassis Ital Design created a compact body marked by simple and functional lines. It offers excellent visibility for driver and passengers, as well as accessibility and comfort. A novel feature is the wide rubber belt encircling the body of the car, which not only increases general protection but also safeguards the car from damage caused by minor collisions. This reduces maintenance costs.

The following sections describe in detail the technical characteristics with special emphasis on those features which contribute to the comfort, convenience, and protection of driver and passengers.

Passenger Compartment

The rear seat accommodates three people facing forward. Two more can sit on folding seats facing the rear. A folding armrest in the center of the rear seat

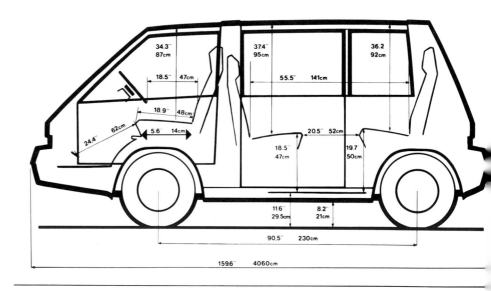

Plan of *Alfa prototype indicating dimensions.*

Diagram indicating location of engine over the wheels.

*Elevation indicating
dimensions and seat
structure.*

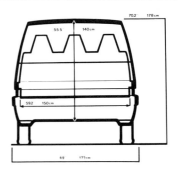

*Elevation showing
passenger accommo-
dation.*

*Elevation and plan
showing dimensions
and driver visibility.*

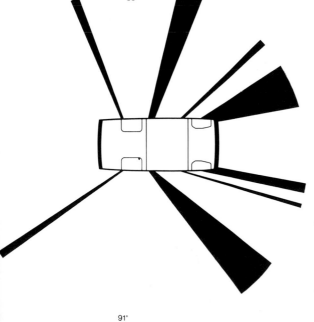

Plan of vehicle interior showing space for additional passengers.

On the curb side is a sliding door with a retractable ramp which can accommodate carriages and wheelchairs.

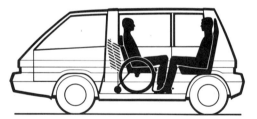

Plan indicating the actual positioning of wheelchair in the interior space.

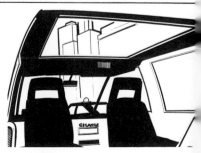

Rendering of interior space showing tinted glass roof which increases visibility and reduces glare.

Extra space for baggage is available at the right of the driver's seat.

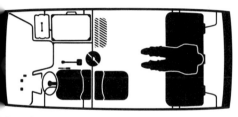

Plan of seating accommodations.

adds to comfort when there are only two passengers.

All seats are equipped with safety belts and compact headrests which do not impair visibility. Upholstery is washable for easy maintenance and "breathes" for comfort in hot weather.

Anatomically designed seats afford correct seating position and provide support. When the vehicle is at a standstill, the seats are relatively firm; in motion they not only absorb vibrations, being harmonized with the suspension, but also become more comfortable as their flexibility becomes more effective with speed.

The baggage area is located adjacent to the front passenger seat. Enclosed by a vertical retaining lip, the baggage area is covered with a special non-slip material. The rest of the floor is covered with practical rubber. To further prevent baggage from shifting, a push-button control operates a vertical restraining device. Extra space for baggage is available to passengers at the right of the driver. Because the floor is only 11.65 in. (29.5 cm.) from the ground, the Alfa taxi facilitates entry and exit of passengers and handling of luggage.

Another feature is the sliding door on the curb-side which leaves the door opening completely free even in the most confined parking situations. The usable area of each opening is 35 in. (89 cm.) wide and 53 in. (135 cm.) high. A retractable ramp under the floor can be quickly pulled out to pro-

vide easy entry and exit for baby carriages and wheelchairs. The sliding passenger door, which opens from both inside and outside, can be equipped with an electrical locking mechanism controlled by the driver.

Passenger-area window surface (side and rear) totals 28.4 sq. ft. (2.64 sq. m.). In addition, a large tinted glass roof measuring 39.4 in. (100 cm.) by 31.5 in. (80 cm.) affords extra visibility, with a sunshade to block glare.

Total passenger-compartment area—from partition to the back of the rear seat—measures 68.5 in. (174 cm.). This is larger than in any taxi built on a sedan chassis; it is even larger than in the famed London taxi, which offers a passenger area 47 in. long (118 cm.) in a total vehicle length of 140 in. (357 cm.), as against the 160 in. (406 cm.) length of the Alfa Romeo prototype. Usable floor space in the passenger area is 20.4 sq. ft. (1.90 sq. m.).

A bulletproof safety-glass partition separates the passenger and driver compartments. A two-way intercom provides communication. Fares are collected via a pivoting receptacle in the partition. The meter is placed in the driver's compartment, in an inclined position visible to passengers.

Driver's Compartment
Special attention has been given to the driving position, with emphasis on comfort, easy operation of controls, and high visibility in order to reduce driver fatigue and promote safe operation of

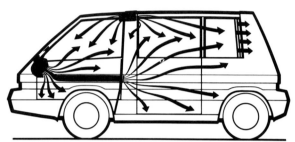

*Heating system and
air conditioner, lodged
under the forward
roll-bar.*

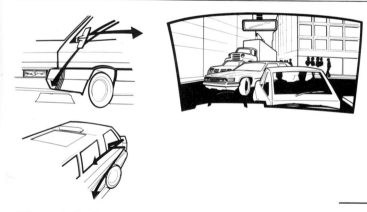

*Diagram indicating
oversized outside rear-
view mirrors.*

*The Alfa Romeo pro-
totype has a mechani-
cal jack positioned at
each wheel.*

the vehicle. Excellent vision is obtained through the large windshield 34.25 in. (87 cm.) high and 50 to 58.25 in. (127 to 148 cm.) wide. Visibility is broadened by the large side and rear windows, the oversized outside rear-view mirrors on both sides, and the heated rear window. All controls are easily operated by the driver. In addition to the usual instruments, the dashboard displays warning lights to indicate whether passenger doors are properly closed. The dashboard is covered with non-glare material.

Next to the driver's seats are two compartments: one is for papers and small items, the other holds the money box and can be locked. Another compartment, for the driver's personal effects, is located at the rear of the vehicle with access via a door under the rear window.

The driving position is favorably located well behind and above the engine, which is over the front wheels. This automatically provides better protection and insulation from vibrations. It also allows a more relaxed driving position—with plenty of room for legs and arms in relation to the steering wheel, pedals, and stick shift—which reduces fatigue. The anatomically designed reclining seat is inclined slightly to the rear and permits needed support for shoulders and kidneys. Firm lateral support is also supplied. The seat is equipped with seat belt and compact headrest, and there is an armrest on the door panel.

Many of the vehicle's features work to make driving easier and less fatiguing: the flexibility of the twin-cam engine

Plan indicates a protective rubber belt, a special safety feature.

makes it adaptable to all kinds of traffic; low center of gravity and independent suspension all around contribute stability and comfort. The sliding passenger door provides convenient access in restricted areas; four mechanical jacks—one at each wheel—make possible rapid raising of the vehicle.

Both the driver's compartment and the passengers' compartment have a single-unit heating system and air conditioner, which are lodged under the forward roll-bar.

Mechanical and Safety Features
The engine is the famous Alfa Romeo 4-cylinder dual-overhead-cam type, with 1290 cc. cylinder capacity, sodium-cooled valves, aluminum-alloy cylinder head and block. Because the engine was developed for high-performance Alfa Romeo cars, its use in a light commercial vehicle ensures excellent performance in difficult urban and suburban traffic conditions. For the same reason, it offers exceptional durability and toughness.

Front-wheel drive features a transaxle, with gearbox integral with differential. There are four synchronized forward gears, plus reverse.

Suspension is independent front and rear, with double-acting telescopic shock absorbers.

Brakes are disc front and drum rear, with power assist and pressure modulator to provide high-efficiency braking in all conditions.

Safety features include a chassis of great structural strength, with a roll-bar above the partition between the driver's compartment and the passenger area. In addition, the roof receives extra strength through a supporting rib running from the skylight to the rear window.

A striking safety feature of the body is a protective rubber belt, 5.1 in. (13 cm.) high and 2 in. (5 cm.) thick, completely encircling the exterior. Besides offering extra protection for the headlights, the belt helps absorb the impact of major collisions. It reduces the effect of minor traffic encounters and parking incidents like side-scrapes, thereby helping to reduce maintenance costs. The bumpers comply fully with U.S. safety regulations. Another body feature is the absence of protrusions to snag pedestrians or other vehicles.

Other important factors contributing to active safety (prevention of accidents) and passive safety (protection in case of accident) include:

1 Protected driving seat.
2 Wide visibility for the driver, since the elevated seat enables him to look out over normal traffic.
3 Two double-size external rear-view mirrors.
4 Heated rear window for de-icing and de-fogging.
5 Dashboard warning signal that tells driver whether passenger doors are open or closed.
6 Front signal lights that are easily visible, in a high position. Back lights in three colors: green (normal night driving); amber (slow down); red (brakes).
7 High stability and superior road-holding due to low center of gravity, front-wheel drive, and fully independent suspension.
8 Easy, responsive steering that is aided by direct and precise linkage as well as by the maneuverability of the vehicle, which is narrower than the conventional taxi.
9 Sliding passenger door that does not interfere with sidewalk traffic when open.
10 Safety belts and headrests for all seats, driver's as well as passengers'.
   Dimensions of the prototype are:
   Length   13 ft. 4 in. (406 cm.)
   Width   5 ft. 7.75 in. (172 cm.)
   Height   5 ft. 10 in. (178 cm.)

—**Alfa Romeo**

As the floor is only 11.65 in. (29.5 cm.) from the ground, the Alfa taxi facilitates entry and exit of passengers and handling of luggage.

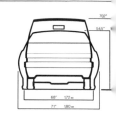

Elevations showing dimensions of Alfa Romeo prototype as compared to a traditional taxi.

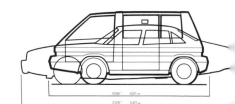

Design
Specifications
Manual

A taxi conceived specifically for meeting urban traffic conditions represents a matter of considerable importance in improving the quality of life in the urban environment, and the research along these lines is an important aspect of the design activity. Such a vehicle must present outstanding properties of emission control, high maneuverability, driver comfort and safety, as well as adequate and comfortable accommodations for passengers and luggage. Moreover, it must also be endowed with certain basic characteristics such as compact external dimensions, generous ratio between overall size and usable space, good accessibility, ease of employment, visibility, handling, high safety margin, easy identification.

Recognizing the requirements of urban mobility and the absence of appropriately designed automotive means to satisfy such needs, The Museum of Modern Art, through its Department of Architecture & Design, proposed and organized the Taxi Project. The Taxi and Limousine Commission of New York City, in close cooperation with the Museum's staff and its engineering consultants, and in consultation with the representatives of New York City Taxi Fleet owners and private taxi owners, prepared the following Design Specifications Manual for an improved taxi vehicle.

This taxi is intended to provide an appropriate "matching" of transport capability to payload by optimization for two to three passengers, while retaining the full load capacity of four. It shall thus provide a fuller level of comfort for two to three passengers, and acceptable through perhaps reduced levels of comfort for four. Appropriate levels of safety shall be maintained for all occupants.

The taxi shall incorporate the highest practical interior to exterior cube ratio, with the lateral dimension in particular being reduced (that is, closer to the London Cab's 60 in. width than the current American stock sedan's 70-80 in.). Compactness will reduce the spatial impact on downtown environments, and the reduced lateral dimension, insofar as it does not critically detract from road-worthiness, is intended to increase traffic penetration capability.

The taxi design must meet with established federal Motor Vehicle Safety Standards (MVSS), and insofar as is practical with the intent of proposed MVSS except where the latter is clearly at variance with the Project's aim of creating an improved urban taxicab. *It is intended that the taxi shall represent one variant of a second type of urban vehicle; and further, the Project will propose that the federal National Highway Traffic Safety Administration (NHTSA) recognize this second type of urban vehicle as better suited to highway use than the standard, heavier, and larger type of car.*

Engineering analysis on road-worthiness and crash-worthiness consistent with that normally required for meeting federal MVSS certification will be important to insure that these performance categories have not been unduly compromised in meeting the special requirements of this Project. At the present time, however, neither category has been very much developed in terms of actual MVSS requirements. Further, it is recognized that insofar as the Project requirements as stated herein tend away from the low-profile "race car" styling common in standard vehicle design, they will tend to a certain degree to reduce road-worthiness performance. Similarly, the current crash-worthiness philosophy found in much of the safety literature tends to surround the passengers with a great bulk of car body for maximum energy absorption in highway speed collisions. Thus, the special requirement of this Project, of high inner-to-outer cube effectiveness, militates against current trends in safety. The dilemma is clear: The taxi prototype design must develop appropriate levels of safety, while still providing a vehicle of reduced impact on its environment. As stated above, it is therefore contemplated that such a design will form the spearhead of a second type of vehicle to be recognized by evolving MVSS standards, which establishes a different trade-off between economy, ecology and safety: a new type of vehicle appropriate for semi-public use in congested urban quarters.

It is the intention of the New York City Taxi and Limousine Commission (TLC) to test the prototypes submitted in actual taxi service. Those prototype vehicles found suitable for the rigorous demands of taxi service will be used to guide the establishment of standards which all taxicab designs must follow in order to be approved for use in New York City after 1978. The Commission will, therefore, direct the testing and field demonstration in actual taxi service of prototypes resulting from this Project.

The Taxi Project
The standards promulgated here are stated essentially in terms of *performance,* in order to allow the designer and manufacturer maximum leeway in achieving the highest level of design. The document describes general design characteristics to be satisfied and gives certain specific dimensions and requirements that constitute appropriate minimums for the design of the taxi. Careful

distinction has been made in the text when using the terms "must" and "should." "Must" items are considered mandatory, while "should" items are felt to be highly desirable although not strictly mandatory.

1.1 *Accommodations*
The Taxi Project has developed a passenger accommodation philosophy based on transit vehicle design recognizing four basic loading modes:
1. empty
2. seated
3. standees
4. crush

Similarly, the taxi accommodation entails two loading modes:
1. normal
2. 'squeeze' loading

The normal loading mode accommodates two to three passengers at optimum sedan seating levels of comfort; and the 'squeeze' mode accommodates up to four with the use of supplemental seat arrangements.

1.2 *Luggage*
Applying the same design philosophy to the accommodation of passengers' luggage will imply that participating companies seek double utilization of space. Essentially this means that the secondary, or squeeze accommodation places will be used for luggage when not occupied by persons. The economic/ecologic mission of the taxi is deemed to be such that it should not be designed to accommodate ultimate loadings of a maximum number of passengers plus a full complement of luggage but rather, an either/or type of capacity. At the same time, however, the vehicle shall be designed so that passengers may load and off-load their luggage easily themselves.

1.3 Seating, Support and Restraints (see also 1.6.1)

1.3.1 Crash Safety
The two or three primary seating positions must incorporate an appropriate complement of proven energy attenuation and occupant restraint devices, and, as a minimum, must meet current FMVSS requirements.

1.3.2 Seat Design (Primary)
The seat back rest should have its lower edge 1 to 2 in. above the H point to ensure good lumbar support and provide a recessed trough for seat belt hardware. There must be contact between the installed manikin back-pan and the seat back rest, up to 21 in. above that point on the centerline of the back-pan, closest to the H-point. There must also be contact between the installed manikin seat-pan and the seat cushion for a distance of 11.5 to 12.5 in. from directly beneath the H-point and forward along the seat-pan's centerline. The seat cushion should be firm at its forward edge so that it is supportive at its full 13 in. height above the floor when the occupant has slid forward and is about to step out.

1.3.3 Head Restraints
A head restraint mechanism must be provided for each primary position. Since such restraints may offer severe obstructions to the driver's view, innovative solutions are encouraged. Concepts utilizing the basic vehicle interior architecture will be considered. For example, padding may in some cases be attached directly to the partition or backwindow, if their feasibility can be understood in terms of requirements 2.5.1.8 and 2.5.1.9.

1.3.4 Supplemental Seats
Supplemental seats will be designed and/or protected with cushions so that they present a minimal hazard to the occupants of the primary seats, when they are in the deployed position. Seat belts must be provided for each supplemental seat position, and the seat must be designed to be pulled easily into its deployed position with the belts and seat remaining anchored and effective.

1.4 Driver-Passenger Separation
It is assumed that the security requirements of the driver will lead to a high degree of environmental separation of passengers from the driver. Indeed, past experience with partitions has shown that the problem is one of improving communications between the two sides of the partition. Both speech and the exchange of money have been significantly impeded. It is intended that Taxi Project vehicles will provide solutions to this problem.

1.5 Comfort and Convenience
The interior of the compartment must be designed to be attractive, easy to maintain, and durable.

1.5.1 Climate Control
Provision must be made for heating, fresh air ventilation, and air conditioning (optional) for all occupants. Separate controls of fresh air should be provided (apart from the opening windows) for both passenger and driver compartments.

1.5.2 Ashtrays
Theft-proof, easy-to-clean ashtrays must be included. They must not be installed in the front seat backrest, however.

1.5.3 *Passenger Lighting*
There should be acceptable sources of illumination within the passenger compartment which do not unduly obscure the vision of the operator.

1.5.4 *Armrests*
A folding armrest at least 6 in. wide should be incorporated at a location between the two primary seating locations in addition to door-mounted armrests.

1.6 *Dimensions*

1.6.1 *Seating and Measurement Methodology*
The following dimensions are meant to be used with conventional types of bench seating, 'bucket' and folding seat designs. The dimensions specified are meant to provide a high level of seating and interior comfort. They must be followed if such conventional seating types are adopted by the designer and manufacturer. *This Project, however, does encourage innovative passenger seating design if it improves comfort and safety. Consequently seats of other than the conventional design may be provided if they meet the required dimensions or the intent thereof.*

Interior measurements will be made in accordance with the Society of Automotive Engineers (SAE) Aerospace Automotive Drawing Standards, Section E-1; except for GM-H69, a General Motors standard which is defined herein; and which has been proposed to the SAE by GM to become an SAE standard; and TA, SR, HR, EnW, and ExSW, which are special TLC measurements defined herein; or any modifications of these methods made subsequent to the writing of this document. All measurements of passenger and driver accommodations must be made with a three-dimensional manikin

using 95-percentile male dimensions, as described in the SAE Recommonded Practice J826a.

1.6.2 *Primary Passenger Accommodations (fixed in position)*

1.6.2.1 *Seats*—The primary passenger seating must be capable of comfortably accommodating two passengers and should accommodate three.

1.6.2.2 *Cab Floor*—Should be flat for an area of at least 48 in. wide and 25 in. fore and aft irrespective of jump seat assemblies.

1.6.2.3 *Roof Liner*—Should be at least 54 in. above the floor over the 48 x 25 sq. in. area.

1.6.2.4. *Foot Angle*—Rear (SAE L47)—must be between 110° and 120°. A suitable footrest will be provided to accommodate all sizes ranging inclusively from the 5 percentile female to the 95 percentile male. By doing so L47 will, in no case, be less than 90° nor more than 120°.

1.6.2.5 *Minimum Effective Leg Room*—Rear (SAE L51) should exceed 45 in. and must exceed 40.

1.6.2.6 *Knee Room*—Rear (SAE L48)—must exceed 10 in. when primary seats alone are in use.

1.6.2.7 *Effective Head Room*—Rear (SAE H63)—must exceed 40 in.

1.6.2.8 *The Head Swing*—(TLC-HS)—must equal or exceed an arc of 33.0 in. and should equal or exceed 36.0 in. TLC-HS is measured by an arc radius centered at the H Point and swung from 8° aft of the vertical, backward to the torso line. This arc must clear the headliner, roof structure, and rear window trim.

1.6.2.9 *The Thigh Angle—*
(TLC-TA)—must be between 60° and 70° (TA equals Hip Angle L43 minus Back Angle L41).

1.6.2.10 *Hip Room Rear—*
(SAE-W6)—must be at least 58 in. where a conventional bench seat for three passengers is used. With novel seating, it must be at least 20 in. for each primary occupant.

1.6.2.11 *Shoulder Room—*
Rear (SAE-W4)—must be at least 58 in., with conventional bench seat for three passengers. With novel seating, it must be at least 22 in. for each primary occupant.

1.6.2.12 *Seat Chair Height—*
Rear (SAE-H8)—must be between 12.5 and 13.5 in. This measurement must hold for 8 in. to either side of the occupant's centerline.

1.6.2.13 *The Seat Depth—*
(SAE-L16)—must be no less than 18 in.

1.6.3 *Passenger Accommodations—Supplemental Seat Places*
The following constraints should govern the supplemental seating design:

1.6.3.1 *Minimum Effective Leg Room—Supplemental* (SAE L51s)—must be at least 37 in.

1.6.3.2 *Knee Room—Supplemental* (SAE-L48s)—must be at least 4 in.

1.6.3.3 *Effective Head Room—Supplemental* (SAE-H63s)—must be at least 38 in.

1.6.3.4 *Back Angle—Supplemental* (SAE-L41s)—must be at least 12°.

1.6.3.5 *Hip Angle—Supplemental* (SAE-L43s)—must be at least 90°.

1.6.3.6 *Hip Room—Supplemental* (SAE-W6s) and *Shoulder Room—Supplemental* (SAE-W4s)—must be at least 19 in. for every person to be so accommodated.

1.6.3.7 *Seat Chair Height—Supplemental* (SAE-H8s)—must be at least 12.5 in.

1.7 *Accessibility Requirements*

1.7.1 There must be a passenger door on each side of the vehicle.

1.7.2 The vehicle must be comfortable and convenient to enter and exit.

1.7.3 Adequate provision must be made to allow the handicapped, including those in wheelchairs, to enter and exit.

1.7.4 There must be an assist strap conforming to the impact requirements of Federal Motor Vehicle Safety Standard 201. It may double as a door pull, but its primary purpose is to aid passengers in bracing against sudden stops, and to help entering and leaving the taxi.

1.7.5 The effort required to open and close the passenger doors must be minimized, and the exterior and interior door controls must be easily recognizable, comfortable and convenient to operate. Each door must be equipped with a hold-open latch.

1.7.6 There must be a rain gutter over each door.

1.7.7 Doors must not be hinged at their trailing edge.

1.7.8 The body contour should be shaped to minimize the accumulation of road dirt at the passenger doorways.

1.8 *Accessibility Dimensions*

1.8.1 *Sill Height—*
The door sill should be no higher than the level of the cab floor which should form a fully level surface flush with the door sills.

1.8.2 *The Upper Body Opening to Ground*
(H51) must be no less than 52 in.

1.8.3 *Entrance Height—*
(H12) must be no less than 31 in.

1.8.4 *Exit Height*
(GM-H69) must be no less than 31 in. Exit Height is the vertical dimension measured from the rear H Point to a point on the upper trimmed body opening. This point is located at a station 10 in. forward of the intersection of the side trimmed body opening with a horizontal plane 19 in. above the H Point.

1.8.5 *Entrance Width*
(TLC-EnW) must equal or exceed 22 in. Entrance width is a true horizontal measurement from a point "X" on the foremost edge of the trimmed "C" pillar to the nearest surface of either the held-open door (with the window raised), the "B" pillar, or the partition, if any. The point "X" on the "C" pillar is established as follows: First locate the highest point of the rear doorway's trimmed opening. Then measure 8 in. along a vertical axis below this point. From there, proceed along a horizontal axis to the fore-most edge of the trimmed "C" pillar. The point marked "X" is where the horizontal axis intercepts the "C" pillar trim.

1.8.6 *Exit Shoulder Width*
(TLC-ExSW)—must be no less than 22 in. Exit shoulder width is the distance from the foremost edge of the trimmed "C" pillar 9 in. above the H Point to the nearest surface of either the held-open door with the window raised, the trimmed "B" pillar, or the partition, if any.

1.8.7 *The Entrance Foot Clearance—*
Rear (L19) must be at least 15 in.

2 *Driver Requirements and Safety*
Taxi driving in a congested traffic environment over an eight to twelve hour shift is arduous and sometimes hazardous. The driver must be accommodated in his own separate environment to insure safe and efficient operation. The driver's compartment is his office for long hours of work, and should, therefore, be as functional and comfortable as possible, in order to maximize accident avoidance, or pre-crash safety.

2.2 *Security*

2.2.1 *Driver's Compartment*
The driver's compartment must be capable of providing full isolation from passengers. The vehicle, however, may include the option of allowing the driver to change the degree of isolation to less than complete if the driver so chooses.

A partition shall provide separation between the driver's and passenger's compartments, and shall be capable of stopping a .45 A.C.P. bullet. That portion above the seat back must be fully transparent. Lower portions behind or otherwse adjacent to the driver's seat shall integrally incorporate a 0.045 in. thick sheet of ballistic steel (Mil-A-13259).

2.2.2 *Safe Deposit Box*
Provision must be made for the installation of a safe deposit box to be used by the driver for deposit of fares. Additional provisions for the convenient safe passing of currency and change through the partition must also be included.

2.3 *Comfort, Convenience, and Crash Safety*

2.3.1 *Seat*
The driver shall be provided with a 'bucket'-type seat designed according to accepted human factors and safety criteria. It must incorporate a restraint system conforming to current MVSS standards as a minimum. Designs may, however, show more advanced systems which fully recognize the unique requirements of a cab driver in terms of his relatively stationary position vis-a-vis other occupants, his higher risk exposure, due to time in service, and other factors related to urban traffic environments. The driver's seat should be provided with at least one and preferably two armrests.

2.3.2 *Power Assists*
The need for power assists presumably will be minimized by the reduced vehicle size contemplated. Justifications for such option choices by the entry will be required, with particular reference to the demanding, many-hour shift nature of the driver's task as contrasted with that of the ordinary driver.

2.3.3 *Transmission*
The taxicab must have an automatic trans-mission with a conveniently located control mechanism.

2.3.4 *Operation and Maneuverability*
Operation and handling must be convenient and efficient. The minimum turning diameter should be 28 ft. or less, curb to curb, and must be 35 ft.

2.4 *Dimensional Requirements*

2.4.1 *Back Angle—Front*
(SAE-L40)—must be adjustable from 12° to 28° in increments of one degree or less.

2.4.2 *Effective Head Room—at Centerline of Occupant*
(SAE-H61)—must be at least 40 in.

2.4.3 *Steering Wheel to Thigh*
(SAE-H13)—must be at least 4 in.

2.4.4 *Effective Leg Room—Accelerator*
(SAE-L34)—must equal or exceed 42.5 in.

2.4.5 *Shoulder Room—Front*
(TLC-SR)—must be at least 28 in. The minimum lateral dimension between interior belt moldings or other limiting trim or other limiting surfaces (such as his door) to either side of driver.

2.4.6 *Hip Room—Front*
(TLC-HR)—must be at least 25 in. The inside horizontal dimension measured through the H point between finished trim surfaces to either side of driver.

2.5 *Pre-Crash Safety (Accident Avoidance)*

2.5.1 *Driver Vision*

2.5.1.1 The upper partition, in addition to being of fully transparent material, must be designed so as to hold obstructions to a minimum. It should also be installed at such angles as to minimize reflections that interfere with driver's lateral or rearward view at night.

2.5.1.2 The roof support pillars must be designed so as to provide the minimum obstruction to the driver's field of vision.

2.5.1.3 The driver should be able to see the body perimeter up to the extremities of the body and bumper, within tolerances measured in a horizontal plane of 3 in. laterally and 6 in. fore-and-aft.

2.5.1.4 The sun visors should permit the driver to obscure all of that part of the windshield which lies above the horizon as seen from the lowest point in the 95 percentile eye-ellipse.

2.5.1.5 There should be a no-glare surface on the dashboard below the windshield and surrounding the instrument panel.

2.5.1.6 All relevant elements of the vehicle should be designed to insure satisfactory rearward vision.

2.5.1.7 The rear-view mirrors, inside and outside-left, must meet the requirements of SAE Recommended Practice J834a and should exceed them in the horizontal plane by a margin of 100 per cent.

2.5.1.8 The eye-ellipse should be positioned at an elevation to assure a maximum of vision through other vehicles in traffic. Current practice has accomplished this largely through the relatively standard geometry of sedan windshields and rear windows. Where novel vehicle types such as light van-type vehicles are considered, they should attempt to achieve an equal "see-through" vision capability by placing the eye-ellipse at an elevation sufficiently above standard sedan roof heights.

2.5.1.9 *Alternative A*
A sedan back window must be either vertical or tilted aft of vertical by a small angle. A van window must be tilted backward at a slight angle.

Alternative B
The back window must be concave around either a transverse axis or a vertical axis.

In both cases, the aim is to assure that the brightness of the sky will not be reflected back towards following vehicles. The objective here is to improve through-vision, thus giving the driver advance information of traffic movement ahead (as discussed in 2.5.1.8. above).

2.5.2 *Maintenance of Driver Vision*

2.5.2.1 The windshield wipers should have an intermittent mode of operation, in addition to slow and fast speeds.

2.5.2.2 The rear window must have a defogging system meeting the requirements of SAE Recommended Practice J953.

2.5.2.3 Where the vehicle design does incorporate a cantilevered rear trunk at the rear of the vehicle, the upper surface(s) shall be painted a black of a low specular gloss.

2.5.2.4 Where the vehicle design does incorporate a forward-projecting hood in the vehicle design, the upper surface(s) shall be painted a black of low specular gloss.

Of the two previous requirements, the first is intended to minimize the loss of rearward and lateral vision in moist or rainy conditions where unwiped droplets act as prisms reflecting the yellow of the trunk deck. The second is to reduce sun glare where there is a forward-projecting hood at the front of the vehicle.

2.5.2.5 The headlamps must be incapable of retraction or concealment.

2.5.3 *Special Display Information*
A door-ajar warning light must be installed in plain view of the driver. A red warning lamp should be installed adjacent to each passenger door. It must turn on whenever the door is unlatched.

2.5.4 *Rear Signal Lamps*

2.5.4.1 Rear signal lamps must be located either on the roof along the 'B' pillar station line to either side of the taxi roof light, in which case front signal lamps will be located coincidentally. The roof 'B' pillar station line location has been used for emergency vehicle beacons, and was instituted for use by the NYC TLC 1973 taxicab specifications with wide and rapid acceptance in the industry. This requirement is intended to maximize through-visibility of signals.

2.5.4.2 Rear signal information must include green for running under power, amber for slowing under engine compression, and red for brake application, in addition to those required by MVSS. Accessory kits incorporating the above functions have been available for some time. While such equipment duplicates some functions presently required, it is anticipated that the significant improvement in information provided, if demonstrated by use in a particular vehicle population, could eventually supplant the

established red running, red braking system, since the latter requires a high level of discrimination to determine whether vehicles at a distance ahead are moving or stopped, often creating hazardous conditions.

2.5.5 *Controls*

2.5.5.1 All controls for vehicle operation and for the comfort of the driver must be placed so that he can reach them easily with his seat belt and shoulder harness fastened.

2.5.5.2 Within convenient reach of the driver there must be at least two compartments, one open and one with a locking lid, for his personal articles. Their combined volume should not be less than one cu. ft.

2.5.6 *Signalling Devices*

2.5.6.1 The front and rear side marker lights required in federal MVSS 108 should flash when the turn signals are flashing. The various lamps that flash in the turn signal system need not flash on simultaneously, but all lamps must individually meet requirements of paragraph 2.5.6.3. (below) for flashing rate and per cent of time "on."

2.5.6.2 The primary turn signal lamps must flash "on" immediately when the control lever is moved.

2.5.6.3 The flashing rate, with all turn signal lamps functioning, should be between 60 and 120 flashes per minute and the per cent of time current flows must be between 30 and 75 per cent when the system is tested, in accordance with the requirements of MVSS 108. (Reference: The Auxiliary turn signal lamp called for in the Owner's Rules specifies a 21 candle-power bulb).

2.5.6.4 The turn signal control lever must have a spring-loaded "off" position to flash the lamps for a lane change.

2.6 Vehicle Identification and Signage

2.6.1 *Taxi Color*
The taxi exterior should be painted primary yellow except on certain parts of the body (see Section 2.5.2.4.).

2.6.2 *Taxi Light*
A highly visible taxi light of approved design must be installed on the roof near the 'B' pillar station line. The light is to be triggered by the operation of the taximeter. The wiring must be inaccessible to tampering.

2.6.3 *Taximeter*
Provision must be made to install an approved taximeter in a location readily accessible to the driver and its readout in full view of the forward-facing passengers. The meter must not interfere with the driver's safe operation of the cab or the passenger's safety and comfort.

3 Vehicle Design and Crash Safety Features

3.1 *Injury Reduction*

Occupant safety must be studied with particular reference to reduced vehicle size. The normal vehicle mix will continue to place smaller, lighter vehicles at a disadvantage because of the higher acceleration values their passengers will experience in collisions with heavier vehicles.

This will be particularly problematical in the case of van-type vehicles. Very short front and rear body sections fore and aft of the passenger cabin may require novel alternative strategies to accomplish the necessary attenuation of deceleration due to collision. Hydraulically actuated energy-absorbing extendable bumpers may be necessary. It may also be necessary to consider higher than currently accepted levels of cabin structural displacement. A controlled mode of collapse designed to be fully compatible with human factors, particularly with respect to folding and hinge points, may facilitate some additional attenuation not possible with current "strong-box" philosophy. Even with such approaches, it may be necessary to speed-limit such vehicles for different situations in order to assure acceptable levels of crash deceleration. It should be noted that this problem has been recognized as being generic to the light van-type vehicle. The aim of this discussion is not to discourage, but rather to encourage such vehicles, and to urge the investigation of approaches to overcome these problems, since such compact vehicles are considered highly desirable to the aims of the Taxi Project. The Project encourages innovative approaches to this problem. However, such approaches should not interfere with the performance called for in Section 3.2., Cost Reduction Requirements.

3.2 *Cost Reduction Requirements*
Participating manufacturers must recognize that normal taxicab operation in dense urban traffic environments involves a very high incidence of light brushing side contacts and corner impacts, as well as a higher incidence of rear and front collisions than that which privately operated cars experience. Designs must therefore seek every practical means of reducing costs to operators stemming from operation in such an environment.

3.2.1 *Exterior Geometry*

3.2.1.1 Vehicle corners front and rear should incorporate the largest practical radius(ii). In the case of the front corners, the geometry shall be such that the vehicle should fully clear or not extend beyond the vertical plane prescribed by the outside front wheel, when the vehicle is making a minimum radius turn.

The aim of this requirement is to reduce the likelihood of vehicles contacting other vehicles while maneuvering in congested traffic, and to minimize damage costs where such contacts do occur through the maximized deflection characteristic inherent in the geometry specified.

3.2.1.2 *Front End Upper Surfaces*
The vehicle front must be curved, smooth and free from hard edges or projections which might cause injuries to pedestrians.

3.2.1.3 *Door and Quarter Panel Design*
That portion of doors and quarter panels lying in the fully vertical plane must be maximized. Rub strips and resilient materials to minimize surface and finish damage costs should be incorporated within the vertical exterior body area.

The aim of this requirement is to reduce body work and finish repair deriving from light to moderate side contact with other vehicles by exposing broad flat areas of contact between vehicle sides which are intended to be geometric and surface-material-compatible.

3.2.2 *Bumper Design*
Bumper designs must meet the requirements of FMVSS standard 215. The aim of this standard is to insure the preservation of the vehicle's safety-related operating equipment in 5 mph front or rear contact with other cars, and to reduce frequency of bumper override in higher speed collisions. Vehicles must additionally meet the following Taxi Project bumper requirements.

3.2.2.1 *Increased Bumper Height:*
The bumper vertical measurement must be increased to add 4 in. to MVSS requirement, with the additional increment to be added below, thus providing coverage between 12 in. and 20 in. above the road surface. The bumper face must be of simple or near simple curvature (not compound) curving about vertical axes at or near the corners of the vehicle. In addition, the bumper must incorporate horizontal ridges running the length of the bumper. There must be two or more such ridges, raised ½ in. or more beyond the bumper face itself. The ridges may be of a resilient material.

A bumper similar to those commonly used on motor buses and delivery vans is contemplated; however novel designs will be acceptable, where it can be seen they will exceed the above-stated requirement. The aim of this requirement is to expand compatibility downward to include doorsills, so as to reduce the likelihood of penetration in side crashes, and to reduce the likelihood of pedestrian overrun as well. The ridges provide an anti-climb function.

3.2.2.2 *No-Hook Characteristic:*
The bumper side portions shall be largely flush with the quarter panels or fenders above them, and shall not protrude excessively beyond the quarter panels. The extremities shall be curved to avoid exposing the bumper extremity so as to snag other vehicles. The aim of this requirement is to minimize bumper hooking on corner impacts in which the

vehicles are pulling away from each other.

4.1 *Vehicle Noise*

4.1.1 The taxicab must meet the requirements of SAE Standard J986a. Furthermore, using the same measuring techniques, it must not generate an A-weighted sound level greater than 76 decibels at 50 ft. when driven at a steady speed of 35 mph.

4.1.2 The noise level inside the taxi, measured at the possible locations of the passenger's head with all windows closed, should not exceed 65dBA at 30 mph and 76dBA at 70 mph.

4.2 *Horn and Alarms*

4.2.1 All vehicles must conform with Section 1403.3-5.17 of Part III of Chapter 57 of the New York City Administrative Code and any other noise control regulations on horns promulgated pursuant to this Section by the City's E.P.A. Administrator.

4.2.2 A back-up warning buzzer should operate whenever the transmission is in reverse. It should generate an A-weighted sound level of 60 to 65 dBA at 10 ft. to the rear. It should not generate a strident or unpleasant sound.

5 *Emissions*

5.1 The engine must run on electric power or other non-polluting forms of propulsion.

A warning light must be installed for the driver to observe in case of failure of advanced emission control devices.

Historical and
Critical Essays

The Role of Taxis in Urban Transportation

Emilio Ambasz

The recent energy crisis has, among other things, brought about a growing interest in the role of the taxicab in urban transportation. Numerous studies and demonstration projects are now seeking to define the scope of the services, real and potential, which taxis can render to the community. Their purpose is to propose ways of improving conventional taxi vehicles and to introduce reforms in the available range of taxi services. Included in the proposals are changes in the present restrictive requirements for private and public financing of the taxi industry, as well as the introduction of new taxi regulations that would be fair to the drivers, the industry, and the public.

But the taxi is not the child of the latest crisis. Its history goes back to the 17th century. Long before any special vehicles were built as taxis, private horse-drawn coaches were already in use for such services. The history of taxi design competitions is also older than generally presumed. As Mr. Georgano notes in his survey, the first competition for a motor-driven taxi took place in Paris, in 1898. Of the 14 entrants, only one had a gasoline engine; the rest were electrically driven cabs. But by 1910 gasoline cabs became the majority. Although the controversy over electric versus gasoline engines for taxi propulsion is not over yet, taxis have, in the meantime, become a key factor in urban transportation.

Approximately 170,000 licensed taxicabs are the only form of public transportation available to more than 3,400 American communities. Professor Wohl's statistics comparing taxis to rail and bus systems show that, without taking into account independent car owners, for whom there are no figures, fleet taxicabs transport, by themselves, close to 40 per cent more passengers than all the U.S. rapid transit combined—a volume representing 60 per cent as many passengers as those transported by all bus transit systems combined. Moreover, while conventional public transportation—bus and rail systems—run on fixed routes, and are designed primarily to serve high-density corridors or to tie together the suburbs and the city, the taxi can provide full coverage to both central city and diffuse suburban settlements in an easy and effective door-to-door manner. In terms of cost-per-service, the taxi is known to serve well the needs of the city's middle class and the suburban dweller. But, if the taxi's importance as a public service were recognized, and if the cab were adequately financed and regulated, it could also be made to serve the needs of the handicapped, the old, and the poor who live around the core of central cities, in areas neglected by rail and bus transportation.

Taxicabs have already proven their worth. But, as any taxi-rider knows, there is considerable area for improvement. Such improvements could include not only specially built taxi vehicles, but an exploration of the urban potential of low-cost systems of public transportation such as jitney cabs, subscription-taxi services, and dial-a-ride taxis. The future may also bring what Mr. Richards in his text observes are already experimental realities: the self-drive taxi and the automatic taxi. The working taxi prototypes illustrated in the first section of this book evidence that a small but enlightened sector of the automobile industry has begun to recognize the market potential of a special taxi vehicle, and is also acknowledging its responsibility in contributing solutions to the traffic problems of our cities.

However, good taxi design, such as we have seen in this book, although a necessary condition, it is not by itself sufficient to ensure the automatic success of a comprehensive public transportation system based on taxis. In addition to new designs, new kinds of taxi-service methods ought also to be introduced, such as shared-riding, jitney cabs, and automatic or radio-operated demand-response systems. The management of taxi fleets is another important aspect of taxi-service operation which could be greatly improved by taking advantage of new, computer-assisted managerial techniques. Moreover, the regulations under which the taxi industry works, and the fare structure and licensing restrictions enforced in many cities should be changed to achieve a formula satisfactory to both the public and taxi workers.

At present the taxi industry, under difficult and rigid controls (affecting public and operators alike), is able to finance its own capital and operating costs, at the same time that it employs almost as many people as all other transit operations put together. If it were recognized, at the Federal level, that cabs provide a mass transit service, which equals if not surpasses that of other public transportation systems now receiving subsidies, it need not be considered anti-American to suggest that a restructured and innovative taxi industry should be eligible for grants under the terms of the existing Urban Mass Transit Act. Under this arrangement low-interest loans could be made available to aid the purchase of specially built taxicabs, thus encouraging the motor vehicle manufacturers to develop this aspect of their production. Moreover, funds could be granted to help set up jitney cab operations servicing low-income areas now poorly served by public transportation. Similarly, funds could be made available to cities interested in increasing the number of licensed taxis, so that this may be achieved gradually, without hurting the present investments of the independent and the fleet owners.

The most seductive feature of any plan to assign to taxicabs a formal role in urban transit resides in the fact that such improvements can be brought about by a comparatively small investment. The impact of such changes would be visible in a short time, and have positive effects throughout the city structure. It would not involve heavy investments in equipment and material, or urban expropriations for motorways and rights of way, with all the concomitant aspects of social disruption common to highway construction in urban areas. An improved and expanded range of taxi services would, moreover, provide a wider set of transit choices. It is clearly the most immediate and economical move which can be taken to improve public transportation in our cities and suburbs.

Historical Survey of the Taxicab

George N. Georgano, the British author, has written twelve books concerned with the history of urban transport. He has edited an encyclopedic *History of Transport* (London and New York, 1972) and has also written extensively on veteran and sports cars.

The history of the private-hire vehicle began long before the first taxicab, which was, by definition, a cabriolet with a taximeter to measure distance. Long before any vehicles were specifically built for public use, people operated pensioned-off private coaches, a practice which extended back to the 17th century. Before this, city streets were so narrow and rough that wheeled transportation of any kind was extremely rare. The first coaches for hire were called hackney coaches (from the French 'haquenée,' a strong horse hired out for journeys) and appeared in Paris and London between 1600 and 1620. These grew in numbers over the next century, and by 1694 there were 700 in London alone (fig. 1). They were mostly 2-passenger vehicles drawn by two horses, one to carry the driver (fig. 2).

Then, in about 1800, there appeared in Paris a much lighter vehicle drawn by a single horse, called a cabriolet. The driver no longer sat on a horse but on the carriage beside the passenger, the first cabriolets being 1-passenger vehicles. They were much faster than the lumbering hackney coaches, and were used by young dandies who were delighted to forgo the relative comfort and safety of a coach for a speedy and adventurous ride. Indeed, some young men boasted of the number of times they had been thrown from a cab. A few 2-passenger versions were made in which the driver sat on an outrigger beside the passengers, but the most successful attempt to accommodate two passengers in a cab was made by a British architect,

Joseph Aloysius Hansom (1803–1882), who in 1834 built a square-framed cab with two side-by-side passenger seats, and a seat for the driver on the roof. On Hansom's original cab the driver was ahead of the passengers, but this made the vehicle front-heavy, so that the shafts weighed severely on the unfortunate horse. An improved model was designed by John Chapman, in which the driver sat at the rear with a little window in the roof through which he could communicate with the passengers. This design remained virtually unchanged until replaced by the motor cab, but despite Chapman's improvements it was always known as a hansom cab. Although pioneered in London and a symbol of the city for many years (British Prime Minister Benjamin Disraeli called it "the gondola of London"), the hansom cab was soon taken up by a large number of cities throughout Europe, though it did not reach the streets of New York until 1890 (fig. 3).

With the coming of cabs the hackney coach soon disappeared. The heavy end of the trade was then catered to by the 4-wheeler cab, called either a clarence after William Duke of Clarence (later King William IV of England) or, more familiarly, a growler (fig. 4). These carried two or three passengers and were pulled by a single horse, the driver on a box ahead of the passengers (fig. 5). An important amenity of the 4-wheeler was that it could carry luggage on the roof, which none of its predecessors had done. With the coming of the railroads 4-wheelers were the recognized means of transportation from stations to hotels or houses, and like hansoms were adopted in cities all over the world. They survived longer than the hansoms, and as late as 1927 there were over 100 plying for hire in London. In 1966, in the southern Spanish town of Murcia, the writer rode in one from the station to his hotel; this was not a tourist attraction like most surviving horse-drawn carriages, but a regular means of transport plying alongside the motor taxis. In warm climates another popular form of hired vehicle was the open 4-seat victoria, and these survive for tourists in many cities including Paris, Rome, Madrid, and New York, but not, surprisingly, London, where there are no horse-drawn passenger vehicles of any description.

The second word of the taxicab's etymology, the taximeter, first appeared under that name in Germany in 1891, but a method of recording mileage had been used 44 years earlier. The 'Patent Mile Index' of 1847, tried out on at least one London cab, consisted of a dial resembling a clock inside the body of the cab, on which the hour hand measured the miles and the minute hand fractions of a mile (fig. 6). The "clock" was connected to the rear axle by a specially calibrated gear train which was fully enclosed to prevent its being tampered with. In 1891 a modern-type taximeter measuring time as well as distance was invented by Wilhelm Bruhn of Hamburg. At first the devices were unpopular with drivers, as they reduced the opportunities for overcharging, and at Frankfurt-am-Main Bruhn was thrown

in the river by angry cabmen. However, the meters were soon in use on hansom cabs in Berlin, Vienna, Paris, Stockholm, and London.

With the invention of the automobile in the 1880s, it was inevitable that sooner or later someone would propose a motor cab. The first recorded example was a German-built Benz, two of which plied for hire in Stuttgart in the spring of 1896, followed by a Roger-Benz in Paris in the fall of the same year. It was hardly surprising that Benz cars were chosen, as they were made in greater numbers than any other car at that time. The first powered cabs to be built as such were the electric hansoms made by Harry G. Morris and Pedro G. Salom of Philadelphia. Like the passenger cars of Morris & Salom, the cabs were called Electrobats, and in many ways reversed the conventional layout of automobiles. As in horse-drawn hansoms, the driver sat above and behind his passengers, about eight feet from the ground. The front wheels, which were larger than the rear ones, drove while the rear wheels steered. Braking consisted of pressure rollers acting against the drive wheels. The first of these unusual vehicles took to the streets of Philadelphia late in 1896, and in January, 1897, the Electrobat arrived in New York. An improved version appeared in the same year with the driver on a box ahead of the passengers, and equal-sized wheels. This still had rear-wheel steering, supposed to be useful for maneuvering in confined spaces, and pneumatic tires without treads. The chief advantage of this cab over the Electrobat was that

5

2 *The "coffin cab," so-called because of the similarity of the body to an up-ended coffin.*

1 *London hackney coach, ca. 1680.*

A variation on the hansom cab, with seats for four passengers and entrance at the rear. This is the "parlour" hansom of 1887.

4 *Horse-drawn 4-wheeler cab, Paris. ca. 1900.*

5 *Stealing rides behind cabs was a popular pastime among small boys, and one which caused Britain's first motoring fatality. This Phil May cartoon appeared in* Punch *in October, 1897, less than a month after London's first electric cabs appeared on the streets.*

passengers were fully enclosed from the elements, although in neither cab was the driver protected, perched high in the air in all weathers, and on duty for anything up to ten hours per day. Late in 1897 Morris & Salom's manufacturing rights were acquired by the Electric Vehicle Company of Elizabethport, N.J., which later made Columbia electric vehicles at Hartford, Conn. (fig. 7, 7a, 7b). As well as the enclosed cabs Columbia made hansoms of modified Electrobat type, with equal-sized wheels and front-wheel steering. These were made in considerable numbers, so that by 1900 there were over 200 electric cabs operating in New York City, and many more in other cities. In fact, at this date more cabs were made than any other single type of automobile. They were not entirely successful because of the high cost of setting up battery exchanging and charging depots and their limited range, but Columbia hansoms were made until 1905, and were in use at least until 1910.

London's first electric cabs were the Berseys, which ran from August, 1897, to the beginning of 1900 (fig. 8). In general appearance they were self-propelled growlers, with the driver on a box in front and a 2-passenger enclosed compartment behind. They had 3.5 h.p. motors which drove the rear wheels by chains, and a speed of 9 mph. The range between battery charging was 30 miles. Twelve Bersey cabs appeared on the streets to start with, soon followed by 13 more, and 50 in 1898. They attracted a great deal of attention from press and public, who praised their silence and smoothness, but after six months' constant use various defects began to show up. Tire wear was much heavier than had been expected, though this was hardly surprising as the same tire (solid rubber) was used for the 2-ton Bersey as for a hansom cab which weighed about 900 pounds. Other problems were similar to those encountered by the American electric cab companies. The limited range was a nuisance, and the operating companies found that their electricity bill for recharging was so high that they set up their own generating plant. The public, which had shown so much enthusiasm for the electrics when they were a novelty, soon returned to the familiar hansom and growler. In 1902 the writer H. C. Moore said, "... while you meet hundreds of people who have had one ride in an electric cab, you come across very few who have had two. It is not because their experience was unpleasant that they have not had a second one, but because it was not so enjoyable as a ride in a horse-drawn cab. Apparently the hansom cab has every prospect of retaining its popularity for another 60 years."

This prophecy was sadly wide of the mark, but at least the hansom outlived the electrics. The London Electrical Cab Company never made a profit on the machines, and in August, 1899, they sold the plant and all the cabs. A few were operated by small proprietors for a further nine months, but by the middle of 1900 there were no electric cabs running in London, and it was to be nearly four years before any other self-propelled cabs were seen in the British capital. Only one of the seventy-five Bersey

cabs made is known to survive, and it can be seen at the National Motor Museum at Beaulieu, Hampshire.

The first competition for motor cabs took place in Paris in June, 1898. There were fourteen entrants, thirteen electrics and one with a gasoline engine; they were four Kriegers, six Jeantauds, one Jenatzy, one Bersey, one Bouhey, and one Peugeot (gasoline; fig. 9). Tests included those for speed, hill-climbing, and braking. One Jeantaud was a hansom, one Krieger an open victoria, but all the others were of the motorized four-wheeler pattern, with the driver ahead of passengers in a closed body. The Peugeot was just as impressive as the electrics, and its ability to put on speed without drastically reducing its range was a valuable feature. Its only drawbacks were smell, noise, and vibration. The reporter said, "After running for several hours there was a perceptible warmth under the cushions which would undoubtedly be an inconvenience in hot weather." One of the last tests was a flat-out run to see how long the batteries would last; the winner was the Jenatzy, which covered 105 km. (65.25 mi.), followed by the Kriegers, which did 90–100 km. (56–59 mi.), and the Jeantaud hansom, which reached 86.5 km. (54 mi.). No prizes were awarded for the overall competition. The Cab Trials were repeated in 1899 and 1900, with many of the same vehicles; the electric cabs were faster than before, but a Panhard gasoline cab was the fastest of them all. This had its engine under the driver's box, so the problem of heat under the passengers' seat was solved.

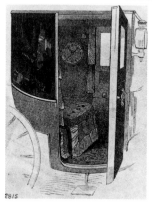

6 The "Patent Mile Index," installed in a cab, 1847.

9 A Peugeot cab similar to that taking part in the 1898 Paris Cab Trials.

Morris and Salom
Electrobats, in front
of the Old Metropoli-
tan Opera House on
39th Street, New
York, 1898.

7a Morris and Salom
Electrobat, outside
Tiffany's in Union
Square, New York,
ca. 1899.

7b An electric cab,
Morris and Salom
Electrobat, New
York, ca. 1900.

London Electric Cab
Company's Bersey,
1897.

In Paris cab operators experienced what they had elsewhere in the world; the silence and smoothness of the electric outweighed its limited range and speed until the motor cab was sufficiently improved. This took place in about 1903–06, and during these years gasoline-propelled cabs began to appear in several major cities. Some tried to adhere to the hansom principle—the British Vauxhall was a true motor hansom steered from the traditional position behind the passengers, while the French Herald had hansom-type doors but with the driver seated in front (fig. 10, 10a). The Vauxhalls, which used the 9 h.p. 3-cylinder inline engine from the firm's passenger cars, were popular with drivers but not with passengers. It was reported that "even to hardened motorists, the apparent rushing straight into danger without being able to see that the driver is doing anything to avert it must be at times disconcerting." Only five ran in London, for less than a year. Other early gasoline cabs were the Rational (fig. 11), with planetary transmission, the Simplex, in which the driver sat in a forward position directly over the engine, and the Pullcar (fig. 12). This was a highly unusual vehicle which had pneumatic tires on its front driving wheels, and solids on the much larger rear wheels. The body was of the hansom type, and could indeed be a genuine hansom modified to fit onto the "half-chassis" carrying the power unit and drive system. In 1906 London had a few Ford cabs, based on the 20 h.p. 4-cylinder Model B car chassis. Some countries, notably Germany, continued to favor the electric cab, though even there gaso-

10a *Royal Cab, hansom style, Paris, 1909.*

11 *Rational cab, London, ca. 1904–05.*

12 *Pullcar front-drive cab, London, 1906.*

10 *Vauxhall hansom cab, London, 1905.*

13 *A German Daimler open victoria photographed in Berlin's Grunewald Park, ca. 1899.*

14 *Bedag electric cab,
Berlin, 1906.*

15 *Darracq cab, New
York, 1910.*

16 *Renault landaulette
cabs in London's
Trafalgar Square, ca.
1910.*

A typical American landaulette cab of about 1910, the Alco. More than a thousand of these cabs were in use in the United States at this time.

line cabs were in the majority. In 1906 Berlin had 439 cabs, of which 89 were electrics (fig. 13). Practically all of these belonged to the Berlin Elektro-mobil-Droschke A.G., and were familiarly known as Bedags (fig. 14).

The nation that really converted the world's cab trade to motors was France, in particular with three makes, Renault, Darracq, and Unic (fig. 15). The Renault was perhaps the best-known of all, appearing in cab form in 1905 (fig. 16). It was a conventional machine for its day, with 9 h.p. vertical twin-cylinder engine, three-speed selective transmission, and shaft drive to the rear axle. As with all cabs of the period, the driver was at first completely unprotected, with neither windshield nor roof, while the passengers were fully enclosed. A feature shared with many cabs was the landaulette top which could be folded down in fine weather. This made cab riding in the park an exceptionally pleasant experience, available to a much wider public than those who could afford a landaulette passenger car. Landaulette cabs were made by Austin in England and Checker in America up to the outbreak of World War II, but after that the additional cost of this type of body, combined with pollution in big cities, spelled the end of the breed. Renault cabs soon became the most popular make in both Paris and London, while the larger 4-cylinder Darracq was adopted in New York. Popular American makes in the years up to 1914 included Alco, Atlas, and Thomas, all with 4-cylinder engines (fig. 17). The first motor cabs

were all 2-passenger vehicles as they were built on relatively low-powered, short-wheelbase chassis. However, from about 1908 onward, four passengers became the rule, usually on 4-cylinder chassis. The additional seats were rear-facing jump seats, and although these were later replaced on many cabs by forward-facing ones, the traditional London cab still has two rear-facing seats today.

In order to keep costs down for fleet operators, the interiors of early cabs were usually Spartan, with no heating or lighting, and cheap leatherette seat covers. However, touches of luxury soon began to appear, encouraged by competition between operating companies. Darracqs had foot-warmers heated by exhaust gases from the engine, while other cabs had electric lights and a speaking tube between the passengers and driver. The 1909 Fiat had an indicator which could be operated by the passengers, showing "Left," "Right," "Faster," "Slower," and "Home," a feature borrowed from private car practice. In general it was the smaller operators who had the smartest vehicles. One of these was Charles McBean of London, who had eight Unic cabs paneled in two shades of green, and in the interior a mirror, ashtrays, and a vase which was filled with fresh flowers each morning.

By 1914 the motor cab was in the majority in all major cities of the world, and had reached a degree of uniformity which is not surprising when one considers that they have to perform basically the same duties whether they are in

London, New York, Buenos Aires, or Sydney. Small 4-cylinder water-cooled engines of up to 2.5 liters (150 cu. in.) displacement were normally used, though Renault still made 2-cylinder cabs, and in America air-cooling was used in Franklin and Frayer-Miller cabs. The driver was likely to have a windshield and roof, though not side curtains or windows (the latter were forbidden on London cabs until 1938), and the 4-passenger body was generally a landaulette. The only electric cab still made in 1914 was the German Lloyd, though quite a number were still in use. Meters were universal in the larger cities.

Few cities, apart from London, had strict rules about the design and construction of taxicabs, and in many, including New York, there were no regulations; any make of passenger car could be used as a cab. London's cab regulations, laid down by the Metropolitan Police, were extensive and strict, dating back to 1906, when the first motor cab rules were drawn up (horse cab regulations dated from 1869). They are worth studying as they represent the most detailed parameters imposed on cab design, and are responsible for the peculiar characteristics of the London cab up to the present day. The internal body height had to be no less than 40 in. (102 cm.) from seat cushions to roof, the width of door no less than 21 in. (53.3 cm.), and depth of back seat no less than 16 in. (40.6 cm.). Length had to be 14 ft. (427 cm.) or less, ground clearance 10 in. (25.4 cm.), and turning circle under 25 ft. (762 cm.) This last rule caused the greatest

headaches to designers, and many cab designs failed this test the first time they were presented. Apart from the tight turning circle there was little difference between a cab and a small town car, so there was no need to make a special chassis. This is why a large number of manufacturers submitted vehicles for the expected motor car boom, although relatively few makes were used in any numbers. Not until after World War I did passenger-car design progress beyond the police limits on matters such as interior height and ground clearance. When this happened the London cab had to be specially designed, more expensive because made in smaller numbers than the mass-produced car. Consequently the number of manufacturers wishing to cater to the cab trade dropped sharply. Between 1905 and 1914 at least 45 British and foreign firms had cabs licensed by Scotland Yard, but between 1920 and 1930 the figure dropped to twelve, and in the next decade to four.

Between 1915 and 1922 two names sprang up which were to become synonymous with the American taxicab business, Yellow and Checker. They were largely the work of two enterprising and far-sighted businessmen, John D. Hertz and Morris Markin. Hertz had worked for the Waldron Shaw Livery Company of Chicago, painting their cabs yellow in order to gain maximum attention on the streets. The first cabs treated in this way were Thomases, followed by Shaw-built cabs, so there were Yellow Cabs a full five years before the actual make appeared. This was in 1915, when Hertz began to produce a conventionally assembled cab using many well-known components, such as a Continental 4-cylinder engine, Schebler carburetor, Tuthill springs, Fisk tires, and American taximeter. The Racine body was a 4-passenger sedan-type with fixed top instead of the traditional landaulette. The Yellow Cab was an immediate success, and was soon taken up by other operators in cities other than Chicago, so that the cabs appeared in various color schemes and with different names on the doors. Design changed little from 1915 to 1921, when a long-wheelbase model was offered: 120 in. (305 cm.) compared with 109 in. (277 cm.). In 1924 a special English chassis was made, with a shorter wheelbase of 99 in. (252 cm.) to comply with Scotland Yard regulations, and a landaulette body, the only Yellow to be so equipped. The short wheelbase combined with the hood length of standard Yellow Cabs gave them a front-heavy appearance, and they were far from the most handsome taxicabs made. Only 120 were built, all in the year 1924. In 1923 Yellow sleeve-valve and Northway air-cooled engines were tried, and the former became widely used in Yellow Cabs until 1926, after which 6-cylinder Buick engines were used (fig. 18).

Yellow's great rival, Checker, began as the cab version of an undistinguished passenger car called the Commonwealth. The cab bodies were built by the Markin Auto Body Corporation headed by a Russian immigrant, Morris M. Markin, and the completed vehicles were sold to a Chicago operator, the Checker Taxicab Company, also a Markin enterprise. In October, 1921, Markin merged his body company with Commonwealth, and soon discontinued passenger car production in order to concentrate on cabs. The first Checkers were generally similar to Yellow Cabs in conception, with 4-cylinder Herschell-Spillman engines and sedan bodies. These two companies were the largest builders and operators of taxicabs, and became involved in the fierce price-cutting war waged on Chicago streets in the 1920s. This became a violent conflict for a while, with cabs being overturned or blown up. Markin's home was also the target of a bomb attack. To help recognize each other, Checker drivers wore on their uniforms and caps the checker trim which also identified the cabs. For a while Yellow also used a Checker pattern on their cabs until they were taken to court by Checker in December, 1923. At this time Checkers destined for New York were built without a right-hand front door as a measure against criminals hiding behind it to rob either the driver or passengers.

In 1924 Checker introduced a landaulette cab alongside the sedan, and in 1927 came a 6-cylinder model, the same year that Yellow launched theirs. Checkers and Yellows were very similar in specification and price at this time, but there were numerous other American taxicab makers in the 1920s. Some were by well-known passenger car makers like Reo, Willys, and Dodge, others were special cab lines by truck makers, such as the Bradfield by Kissel and the Majestic by Larrabee. An unusual survivor from

18 *Yellow Cab Com-*
pany's Metropolitan,
1929.

18a *Rauch and Lang elec-*
tric taxicab, U.S.,
1924.

19 *Beardmore taxi, 1923.*

b *Typical London taxicab of the 1930s. This
is a 1937 Morris Com-
mercial Super Six.*

earlier times was the Rauch & Lang
electric taxi, made in sedan and landaulette forms. Its silent running and the
smoothness of the ride still gave the
electric an edge over the gasoline cab,
but it was very expensive, at $2,875 to
$3,750 compared with $2,185 for a
Yellow Cab.

The year 1929 was a great one for taxicab design; in America both Checker
and Yellow brought out new models,
longer and lower than anything previously made and as good-looking as a
high-priced passenger car, while in Britain a relaxation of Scotland Yard rules
led to a whole new crop of London cabs.
For a long time Londoners had been
complaining that their cabs were high,
boxy, and old-fashioned compared with
passenger cars, but this was inevitable
when the cab designer had to work within the inflexibly prescribed limits.
In 1927 the ground clearance was
reduced to 7 in. (18 cm.), and although the length remained at 14 ft.
(427 cm.), designers brought out
lower cabs nearer the new limit. There
was no major British taxicab maker who
did not bring out a new design between
1928 and 1930. Beardmore, the only
British firm to specialize in cab-making,
launched their Hyper model which was
6 in. (15.25 cm.) lower than its predecessors and had, for the first time on a
London cab, front-wheel brakes
(fig. 19). These had been forbidden
up to 1929 on the grounds that sudden stops might cause accidents and
would encourage cabbies to drive
faster than was necessary. Paris cabs had
front-wheel brakes as early as 1923. At
this time two other manufacturers,

Morris and Austin, entered the cab market. The Austin soon came to dominate the trade because of the reliability and hard-slogging abilities of the Twelve-Four engine. The typical London cab of the 1930s which astonished and delighted American tourists and GIs was generally an Austin; it retained the vertical radiator and windshield up to 1938, making it look a good ten years older than it really was. There was no door or passenger's seat on the near side, but instead a luggage platform capable of accommodating the large cabin trunks popular in the days before air travel. Bodies were supplied by a variety of London coachbuilders, and were nearly all of the landaulette pattern. The last of these cabs did not disappear from London's streets until 1954.

During the 1920s there were a number of attempts in Europe to reduce the cost of taxi travel by using smaller vehicles. In London there was a campaign to popularize the 2-passenger cab, but owners and drivers were against them, and the Home Secretary was persuaded to ban them. A few 2-passenger models did run in other parts of Britain, on such popular small car chassis as Clyno, Morris, and Berliet. For a while the motorcycle-sidecar taxi enjoyed some popularity, seating two passengers either side-by-side or in tandem. They were used in large numbers in Berlin (fig. 20a, 20b) and were also seen in British towns such as Nottingham, Bradford, Cambridge, and Brighton. The fares charged were anything up to 33 per cent lower than for a conventional cab. Germany was the home of

unconventional small cars in the 1920s, and a number of ingenious 1-passenger cabs were tried out (fig. 21). The Hanomag Kommissbrot had a rear-mounted single-cylinder engine of 499 cc. (30 cu. in.) and carried one passenger next to the driver, with a glass panel between them (fig. 22). The Goliath 400 cc. (24 cu. in.) 3-wheeler was made in similar cab form, while in the French Peugeot Quadrilette the passenger was seated in tandem behind the driver. There was even an attempt in France to revive the hansom principle, with a 2-passenger Peugeot coupé driven from a lofty perch at the rear. None of these oddities carried any luggage, and although they were said to be popular with businessmen they did not last long.

By 1930 the specialized taxicab was disappearing in favor of the modified passenger car almost everywhere except for Britain and the United States. The most common Paris taxi of the 1930s was the Renault G7 of which over 2,400 were made, but it was not as distinctive as the London cab. In America Checker built some very handsome machines in the 1930s, including the Series K which so resembled a classic town car that a number of wealthy citizens ordered them for their private use. The Checker Series T featured an eight-in-line Lycoming engine, America's first 8-cylinder taxicab. Yellow's answer to the Series K, which had appeared in 1928, was the O-10, a handsome car powered by a 6-cylinder Buick engine and available as a sedan or town car with open driver's compartment. The latter was known as the Metropolitan, and was finished in a deep

20a *D-Rad, motorcycle taxi, German, 1925.*

20 *A large fleet of motorcycle and sidecar taxis in a Berlin depot, 1926.*

21 *An unusual German cab, the Rumpler of 1924. This had a rear-mounted 4-cylinder engine.*

22 *Hanomag, 1-passenger taxicab, German, 1925.*

23 *General taxicab, with sun-roof, American, 1938.*

24 *The familiar Austin
FX4 London taxicab,
made almost without
external change from
1958 to 1976, and
scheduled for at least
five more years of life.
This is a 1969 model.*

shade of green christened Cellini green after the 15th-century sculptor Benvenuto Cellini. The 1930 models of the Yellow O-10 were renamed General Cab or General Motors Cab—GM had acquired Yellow in 1925 (fig. 23). This marked the end of the Yellow name for cabs, although it survived on buses and coaches until 1944. The 1930 models of the Yellow O-10 and their similar successors the O-12 and O-14 were made until 1934, no GM cabs were built in 1935, and in 1936 the General Cab reappeared as a modified Chevrolet. Wheelbases were nearly 12 in. (30.5 cm.) longer than for passenger cars, and the rear axles came from a Chevrolet truck, but the appearance of the cab was pure Chevrolet. Jump seats were fitted as standard, but a single front seat and partition between front and rear compartments were optional. These were made until 1938, after which the name was changed to Chevrolet. Checker's offering in the immediate pre–World War II era was more original: the Model A used a 6-cylinder Continental engine, and had a streamlined body on which it was surprising to find a landaulette top. Safety features included sponge-rubber head bumpers for the back-seat passengers, and shields to prevent passengers' catching their fingers in the doors. Lights on the dash warned if the doors were not shut properly, or if the gas tank was being overfilled.

Apart from General and Checker, America's cab needs were filled by regular sedans, especially Dodge, de Soto, Plymouth, and Pontiac. They were fitted with sign lights, meters, and optional compartment divisions, but internal space was no greater than in the ordinary family sedan. Ford offered a cab on the Model A chassis (a bargain at $800 in 1929, when a Yellow cost $1,995 and a Checker K $2,500), and some cab bodies were built on Ford V-8 chassis by such firms as Moller of Hagerstown, Maryland, who had built complete cabs of their own in the 1920s.

Just after World War II Checker experimented with rear-engined and front-wheel-drive cabs, the latter with a transverse 6-cylinder engine, but decided against making them in series. When the production Checker appeared it was a conventional 5-passenger sedan with Continental 6-cylinder engine. This Model A2 was developed during the 1950s through successive models up to the A9 of 1958. The A9 featured independent front suspension by coils and power-assisted braking and steering, all innovations for Checker. In style the A9 has hardly changed up to the present day, except for the mandatory heavy-duty bumpers since 1973. Power, however, has been greatly increased, with the adoption of a Chevrolet V-8 engine in place of the old Continental six. Checker cabs have jump seats as standard features, and are much more spacious than any other cabs in service in America today.

In Europe only Britain has built specialized cabs since World War II. As before, Austin has dominated the market. In 1948 they launched their FX3, and replaced it ten years later by the FX4, which is still in production today (fig. 24). The FX3 was lower and longer than prewar models but re-

25 *The 1949 Wolseley Oxford radio taxicab, photographed in a London suburb.*

Checker taxicab of the 1970's, New York.

*Design for the Beard-
more Mark VIII taxi-
cab, 1965, which was
never built. A modi-
fied version called the
Metrocab was made
in 1970.*

*Winchester taxicab,
with diesel engine and
fiberglass body,
London, 1970.*

tained a luggage platform on the curb-
side. The body was pressed steel rather
than the metal panels on an ash frame
of prewar days, and the landaulette
top had been abandoned. An important milestone was the introduction in
1954 of a 2.2-liter (134 cu. in.) diesel
engine as an option for the FX3. Although more expensive to buy than a
gasoline engine, its lower operating
costs outweighed this, and within a year
Austin's London agents were selling
nine diesels to every gasoline-engined
cab. The FX3 broke new ground in that
it was exported in some numbers, about
700 going to Spain, Sweden, Denmark,
Eire, Iran, and New Zealand. Total production of the FX3 was close to 10,000.
In 1958 it was replaced by the FX4
which had a near-side front door for the
first time and could seat three passengers
on the rear seat, which, with two jump
seats, gave a capacity of five passengers.
Scotland Yard regulations have, however,
restricted it to carrying four when operating in London. As with its predecessor
a diesel engine was available. Other innovations on London cabs were independent front suspension and Borg-
Warner automatic transmission. The latter has not been especially popular, as it
is initially more expensive and does not
give such good fuel consumption. Out of
8,725 FX4s licensed in 1970, only 961
had automatic transmission. During its
18-year life span, few changes have been
made to the FX4, although the tinted
glass in the rear window which gave privacy was replaced by clear glass on 1969
and later models. A larger diesel engine
of 2.5-liters (150 cu. in.) was adopted
in 1971. Fewer FX4s were exported

than FX3s, but two were tried experi-
mentally in Philadelphia in 1959, and
one ran in New York in 1968. This was
a gas-engined automatic model tried at
the suggestion of Mayor John Lindsay,
who felt that a smaller cab would be a
solution to traffic congestion. This experiment was conducted by the Yellow
Cab Company (who remained operators long after they gave up manufacture), but they were not very impressed;
even if delivered in a batch of one thousand the cabs would have cost $3,500
compared with $2,700 for the larger
American sedans such as Dodge. And
despite its small engine, the FX4 gave
no better mileage than twelve to the
gallon. The New York public, on the
other hand, was almost unanimously enthusiastic. They praised the easy access
and headroom.

There were several other postwar London cabs, including the Wolseley Oxford
(fig. 25), the first radio cab to operate
on London streets; the Beardmore
(fig. 26), powered by Ford gas or Per-
kins diesel engine; and the Winchester
(fig. 27), which was notable for its fiberglass body. However, none of these has
survived to the present day. The Austin
FX4 seems destined to continue for
many years to come, as the cost of
retooling for a new design is hard to
justify in view of a cab's total sales,
which are not more than 1,500 per year
in London.

In the countries of the Middle East and
Asia, a popular form of taxi is the motor
rickshaw, derived from the pedal-pro-
pelled rickshaw which still survives,

though chiefly as a tourist attraction in the same way that horse cabs do in Europe. Most motor rickshaws are based on motor scooters such as Lambretta and Vespa, and can carry two passengers at up to 35 mph. An example was the Helicak introduced in 1970 by P. T. Italindo of Jakarta, Indonesia (fig. 28). Originally powered by a 148-cc. single-cylinder two-cycle engine, the tiller-steered Helicak could seat three passengers plus the driver. In 1973 it was replaced by a larger 3-wheeled cab with four doors, still with the Lambretta engine. This was doubtless underpowered, for in 1975 the Super Helicak, as it was now called, was equipped with a British-built Reliant 4-cylinder engine.

Numerous experimental taxicabs have been built in the past ten years, especially since the world has become so pollution-conscious (fig. 29). In Holland small electric 2-passenger cabs have been tried in which the hirer drives himself, having been issued a special key on a year's subscription. Witkars, as they are called, can be picked up and left at any of the recognized cab ranks. The same idea has been tried in France with ordinary gasoline-propelled small cars. More conventional but practical is the electric taxi launched in late 1975 by Britain's Lucas Organization (fig. 30). This has front-wheel drive from a 50 h.p. CAV motor located transversely at the front of the vehicle, a maximum speed of 55 mph and a range of one hundred miles per charge. It has no hood, and the flat front not only gives better driver visibility than a conventional cab but also results in an overall length 40 in. (102 cm.) shorter than an FX4, for the same internal dimensions. Five Lucas cabs could park in a rank that can hold only four FX4s. Two of these Lucas cabs are undergoing trials in London at the moment.

8 *Italindo Super Heli-*
cak, Jacarta, Indo-
nesia, 1975.

30 *Lucas electric cab,*
London, 1975.

9 *Fiat taxi, 1968,*
designer, Pio Manzú.

The Present Role of Taxis in Urban America

artin Wohl,
ofessor of Trans-
rtation System
anning at Carnegie
ellon University, pre-
ously taught at
.I.T., Harvard, and
e University of Cali-
rnia (Berkeley). He
s served with the
ban Institute, Ford
otor Company, and
e RAND Corporation
d has written some
rty articles.

The goals of urban transportation are too often viewed as reducing *downtown* traffic congestion, improving suburban-to-downtown commuting, and "getting people out of cars into transit." We look too little at the ultimate purpose, which is fast, efficient transportation. The most talked about "means" for reaching our goals usually include the construction or extension of suburban rapid transit lines as well as subsidies for new and existing facilities, transit fare reduction (if not free transit), the banning of automobiles in the downtown area, parking fee surcharges, and congestion tolls for autos. This kind of rhetoric rarely gains us more than heavy capital commitments for new or extended transit lines, new but still conventional buses or rail cars, and heavier transit deficits. Traffic congestion is not reduced; transit service seems little better—at least for most urban dwellers—and the problems of pollution, noise, and energy consumption remain unabated.

What, then, *is* the urban transportation problem? To really understand the critical aspects of that problem—or, more properly, the *set* of problems— and, in turn, the possible solutions, we need to start by looking at patterns of population, employment, and travel in and around downtowns, central cities, and suburbs as they really are and have been. The following observations will provide a common basis of understanding—and perhaps explode some myths.

First, most people in big U.S. cities who work *downtown*—a term defined arbitrarily as the area of most intense em-

ployment—live today where they have always lived, within the central city and not in the suburbs. In New York, for example, even though its suburbs are blanketed with over 700 miles of commuter railroads (and 500 railroad stations), more than 80 per cent of the people who work downtown (i.e., south of 61st Street in Manhattan) live in one of the five city boroughs. In Chicago, whose suburbs are served by more than 400 miles of commuter railroads, roughly 75 per cent of the people who work downtown live within ten miles of the Loop. Similarly, in low-density Washington, D.C., about 80 per cent of the downtown workers live within six miles of the core. These are *not* atypical cases, and the workers they describe are the prime customers of transit systems (especially those of the rail type).

Second, the pattern is similar when the analysis is extended to workers in entire central cities—the term referring to the actual political subdivisions or jurisdictions which are densely populated. Central-city workers tend to live within the central city rather than to commute from the suburbs. In the 33 largest metropolitan areas in the United States, about two-thirds of the central-city workers live within the city limits. In New York City, where the "central city" includes the five boroughs of Manhattan, Bronx, Brooklyn, Queens, and Richmond, the figure rises to almost 90 per cent; in Chicago and Philadelphia, it is about 75 per cent. In cities having smaller land areas the percentages are lower, but still high: over 60 per cent of San Francisco's central-city workers live within the 45 square-mile city limits; in Boston, Washington, Pittsburgh, and Cleveland (whose land areas range from 46 to 76 square miles as compared to 129 to 300 for Philadelphia, Chicago, and New York), from 44 to 50 per cent of central-city workers live in the city itself.

Third, despite the increasing average incomes of households, the number of homes without automobiles available is on the rise. This is true in the case of cities which lack rapid transit systems as well as within those which possess them. In the 33 largest metropolitan areas (i.e., those having a population of one million or more), central-city households without automobiles available increased about 1 per cent from 1960 to 1970; the increase in those cities having rapid transit systems was even higher—about 2.5 per cent. Put in slightly different terms, about 77 per cent of metropolitan-area households without automobiles available were located within central cities in 1970, a decline of only 3 percentage points since 1960. For cities having rapid transit systems, the concentrations—not unexpectedly—are even higher; in these cities, in 1970, 86 per cent of the metropolitan-area households without automobiles available were located within the confines of the city limits. (This percentage dropped only one point from 1960 to 1970). New York City, of course, is the extreme case with 94 per cent.

A fact of perhaps more significance is that the absolute number of households without automobiles available within the central-city portion of our 33 largest metropolitan areas increased just under 1 per cent between 1960 and 1970. In the six central cities having rail rapid transit systems (i.e., New York, Chicago, Philadelphia, Boston, Cleveland, and Newark), the absolute number of autoless households increased even more—about 3 per cent—from 1960 to 1970.

Fourth, U.S. cities now served by rail transit systems (not including San Francisco, which has a new system in operation) have virtually the same central-city populations (i.e., not including suburban residents) today as in the mid-1930s. These cities—New York, Chicago, Boston, Philadelphia, Cleveland, and Newark—had about 15 million central city residents in 1970, 15.3 million in 1960, 15.7 million in 1950, and 14.4 million in 1930. Employment in these central cities has fallen only slightly more than population over the last two decades.

From 1960 to 1970 the (combined) central-city population of the 33 largest metropolitan areas declined only slightly more than 1 per cent, a figure which hardly attests to massive decentralization. (Of course, this is *not* to say that central cities and suburbs during these periods were experiencing the same growth rates or patterns. It simply reports that in absolute numbers central cities have roughly held their own despite massive suburban growth; the substantial absolute decline in transit patronage can hardly be attributed to decreases in central city population or employment).

Fifth, the 1970 employment statistics for the 33 largest metropolitan areas show that:

1 Only 14 per cent of the employees in these metropolitan areas are central-city workers who live in the suburbs (i.e., outside the city limits).

2 Only 10 per cent of the employees in these areas work within the central business districts.

3 Less than 4 per cent of the total employees in these metropolitan areas work in central business districts and live in the suburbs.

Sixth, from 1950 to 1960 rail transit patronage decreased from roughly 2.1 billion to about 1.7 billion passengers, and from 1960 to 1970 the total decreased somewhat less to about 1.6 billion. The reduction in rail transit ridership between 1950 and 1970 was about five times larger than the decrease in central-city population during the same period in the six cities which had rail transit systems. Overall transit ridership—to include bus and other surface transit—dropped even more during these two decades: from 13.8 billion in 1950 to 7.5 billion in 1960 and to 5.9 billion in 1970.

Two analyses of these facts and trends are important in evaluating past and present transit services, services which have been proposed, and other services which have been overlooked.

One: In general, city dwellers—who by far represent the bulk of transit users—have not become much less numerous; they have simply deserted the available transit systems. This phenomenon is especially remarkable in view of the facts that central-city residents (as a group) are the poorest people in a metropolitan area (and increasingly so, relative to suburbanites) and that the number of households without automobiles is increasingly within central cities. In short, the principal market for transit has remained virtually intact, perhaps even increased between 1950 and 1970 especially in terms of riders who may be regarded as captive because they have less freedom of choice.

Two: The suburb-to-downtown commuter—upon whom we concentrate so much attention—even today represents but a tiny fraction of the metropolitan commuter market (perhaps one person in 20, at best). Even the suburb-to-central-city commuter represents only about one-seventh of the over-all metropolitan-area commuter market, a group which is declining as a proportion of the urban work travel force.

The inevitable conclusion is that the decline in transit patronage on both rail and surface transit systems in our largest metropolitan areas during the last two decades must be attributed for the most part to something other than the decentralization of city workers and jobs.

There are those who claim that these trends have developed because of total neglect of rail systems. But that is contrary to the facts: during the period from 1950 to 1970, New York and other cities with rail systems have improved the facilities, extended their coverage, and increased their subsidies. Boston has extended or vastly improved four rail transit lines since World War II. The Cleveland rail transit system has been extended twice since it was opened in 1956. Philadelphia added the Lindenwold line to its system in 1969 and extended another line. Chicago has built or extended five rail lines in the last two decades, and New York has extended or improved two transit lines in the same period. On most of these systems, both the number of revenue vehicle miles and travel speed have increased. But patronage has steadily declined on all of them, except for a brief (but still small) "boom" that stemmed from the recent fuel shortage and except for increases that occurred for a year or so following the opening of extensions or new lines.

Nor is there good reason to expect a different pattern for the new $1.6 billion Bay Area Rapid Transit (BART) system in San Francisco or the $5.5 billion METRO system being built for metropolitan Washington, D.C. In fact, the patronage pattern for such new systems may be even more depressing. New rail transit systems, and the post-war extensions of old systems, tend to reach farther into the suburbs and to have fewer stations per mile than did the pre-war systems, which primarily served central cities and were designed to offer stations within walking distance of as many people as possible.

For example, the average distance between stations on San Francisco's BART system is about two miles, while that on Washington's METRO will be roughly 1.2 miles. By contrast, the average station spacing on the pre-1960 rail transit lines in New York and Boston was about one-half mile and that in Chicago about two-thirds of a mile. About two-thirds of BART's stations and half of METRO's stations will be located outside the central city, scattered widely throughout the suburbs. By comparison, virtually all of the pre-1960 rail transit stations in New York, Chicago, Boston, and Philadelphia were concentrated within the central city or less than a mile from it. The new systems are trying to reach a market very much like that of the commuter railroads, a low-density market of well-to-do suburbanites. It is a very small market to draw upon; and by having stations so far apart the rail transit systems usually force commuters to drive to and from the stations in second cars, which in fact offer those commuters transportation competitive with the rail systems.

In summary, the solutions now being offered to the public transportation problem (such as BART and METRO), however fast (once you get on them) and pretty, are nothing more than 1970 versions of 1870 commuter railroads that tied together the suburbs and the cities. They lack the accessibility and central-city coverage afforded by earlier rail rapid transit. Furthermore, they fail to provide easy-to-reach, door-to-door service for most would-be users; especially for people without automobiles, for people who are physically infirm, and for people who live within central cities, close to downtown.

The New York region is an example of these trends. It has the largest population and the highest density of U.S. metropolitan areas; the area most suitable for extensive, high-capacity rail systems. Its rail transit system includes some 240 miles of grade-separated transit lines with about 500 passenger stations; this system handles about 80 per cent of all the subway trips made anywhere in the U.S. About four of every five New York subway riders are bound to or from Manhattan, and most of those are headed for somewhere south of 61st Street. About 90 per cent of New York's subway riders are New York City residents; about 10 per cent are middle- or upper-income suburbanites. By contrast, the commuter railroads which cover the New York suburbs handle only one-ninth as many daily trips as the city subway system; the railroads' riders are principally upper-income suburbanites who drive to and from the railroad stations.

Even in New York City, where the fact that an automobile can move at all sometimes seems a miracle, the travel trend is clear: during the 1960s, the five-borough population of New York City rose by about 6 per cent. Downtown Manhattan employment increased by about 7 per cent. But subway and elevated patronage fell during the same period by nearly 10 per cent, and commuter railroads lost about the same amount of business. During this period the number of people coming into downtown Manhattan from various parts of New York City fell by about 4 per cent, while the number of people entering the downtown area by taxicab or automobile rose 10 per cent and the number of vehicles entering downtown went up by 20 per cent.

About 85 per cent of personal trips throughout the *metropolitan* New York area are made by private automobile or taxicab. By contrast, only 25 per cent of the people entering *downtown* Manhattan daily do so by car or cab, and during rush hours that figure drops to about 5 per cent. But one should not be confused by the fact that transit travel is so popular during the rush hour; the fact is that Manhattan streets reach a saturation point at rush hours, and almost everybody travels by transit or not at all. In less dense cities, the dominance of the automobile is even more prominent, a pattern which undoubtedly will continue.

These trends of declining transit patronage, increasing vehicle flow, and declining number of people per vehicle are not atypical. They are characteristic of modern, affluent, urban America and of large, medium, and small cities. They make clear the fact that rich and poor alike are turning away from transit, however improved, subsidized, and inexpensive, toward private automobiles and taxicabs, however expensive and however immobilized in traffic.

This trend is sometimes attributed to a "love affair" between metropolitan man and the rubber-tired monster; but it seems likely that the trend has more to do with comfort and utility than with love.

Commuters do not choose the automobile because transit fares are too high or transit service has deteriorated. Indeed, transit service has improved in many respects and is not nearly so expensive as commuting by automobile. Many studies have shown that riders are relatively insensitive to fare increases or decreases of the sort usually invoked or proposed in most cities. Fare reductions do not significantly increase transit usage and they have little leverage for luring automobile commuters into subway cars or buses.

The figures on urban travel say this: people want good transportation service and are willing to pay for it. They know that subways and buses are cheaper than automobiles, particularly for commuting. But they also find themselves more satisfied with their lot in a car, no matter how long they spend stuck in traffic, than in walking through the rain to a subway station and then waiting to ride to a point from which they must again walk. They obviously feel that bumper-to-bumper beats shoulder-to-shoulder.

The urban traveler wants good, door-to-door service which is free from waiting, walking, transferring, and crowding and which provides comfort, privacy, and convenience. And the urban traveler has made it clear that, at the present time and for most urban trips, he will use a private automobile when he can afford it because it comes closer to providing what he wants than any other available mode of travel.

The key issue is service; that, alone, explains the success of the automobile.

Private automobiles and taxicabs, quite simply, can provide attractive and convenient door-to-door service at a price that many travelers are willing and able to pay. The preference for the automobile and against transit is anything but a man-auto love affair; it is a choice for good but expensive service in contrast to poor but cheap service.

Furthermore, the demand is increasingly for better service. The pattern is clear. A commuter moves as soon as he can from transit to a car pool (a ride to work that is second-to-none in terms of the budget) and from a car pool to driving alone. Eventually, if he joins the ranks of the nation's most affluent commuters, he will be able to give up the driving burden while retaining the convenient, flexible, and attractive door-to-door service afforded by the private car: he will be assigned a chauffeured limousine.

Thus far, this paper has been largely devoted to the most-talked-about, traditional transit forms and their role in recent decades. Little has been said directly and explicitly about the taxicab and its role in urban life, present and future.

To begin, it should be recognized that taxicabs are in every sense public transit vehicles; they represent a distinct and important segment of the transit industry. Fleet taxicabs now handle almost 40 per cent more passengers than do all U.S. rapid transit systems combined, and they carry about 60 per cent as many passengers as all bus transit systems. There are no reliable figures for individually owned cabs in operation, though one may guess that they add a significant increment—something close to one-third of the total. As a consequence, it may be estimated that cabs of all kinds provide a mass transit service which rivals, if not exceeds, that of all other transit systems. This heavy usage occurs even though taxi fares average roughly three times more per passenger-trip and about five times more per passenger-mile than those of other transit services.

Though we do not regard taxis as vital in areas having reasonably strong, publicly supported rail or bus transit facilities, statistics show their transit service to be far more than trivial, despite the fact that they operate under numerous onerous controls and regulations. For instance, even with New York's notoriously restrictive taxi regulations, some one million people use cabs daily, as compared with about one-half million using commuter railroads, four million using buses, and 4.5 million using rail transit. In Washington, D.C., a much lower-density city having fairly open entry for taxicabs but nonetheless still burdened by many taxi regulations and controls (which limit the taxi supply and increase the prices), about 100,000 people use cabs daily, a figure which is about one-third the bus transit patronage.

Moreover, the taxicab industry is the only public transportation service (a few private bus firms aside) that pays its own way (including both capital and operating costs) even under rigid and usually deleterious (to the operator and public alike) controls on fares, licensing, and operations. Today fleet taxicabs alone

generate gross revenues almost 40 per cent higher than those of all other surface transit systems combined. Employment in the fleet taxi is almost as large as total employment in all other transit operations combined.

It is the proposition of this article that, given some reasoned tinkering with regulations, pricing, and operation, taxicabs might very well have a profound and lasting impact on transit patronage and lead to reduced automobile commuting. It is also possible to think of ways in which taxis would better serve some urban groups who are served poorly or not at all by existing transit systems.

Most cities now restrict the number of taxicabs in service, either by limiting the number of licenses or by granting franchises to selected fleets and limiting the size of the fleets. Given its size and density, New York City is the extreme case. The city placed a limit of about 12,000 on the number of medallion cabs in the 1930s; these were originally sold by the city to individual or fleet owners for $10 apiece. Chicago and Boston have similar license restrictions, while Washington, D.C., Atlanta, and Honolulu have virtually no restrictions on the number of fleets or cab licenses. In other cities, such as Los Angeles, there are franchise limitations.

Virtually all U.S. cities also regulate fare levels and the way in which cabs can function in one way or another. For example, public agencies or political groups set zone fares or meter rates, and they often set the conditions under which drivers can pick up additional fares while they still have passengers in their cabs. (During the rest of this discussion, the term "shared-cab riding" will be used to describe a taxi operation or jitney-like service which is allowed to pick up additional passengers along the way after an initial rider has started his trip.) Sometimes meter rates are based exclusively on the distance traveled, and sometimes they reflect both the distance and the elapsed time of the trip, registering at a faster rate, for example, in heavy traffic. Sometimes taxi rates vary with group riding or the amount of baggage carried.

This question of regulation is important because the few studies conducted so far show that riders are more sensitive to the availability of taxis than they are to speeds or travel times. Cities with franchising restrictions have the smallest number of cabs and those with no licensing limits have the largest number of cabs per capita; indeed, unregulated cities have more than three times as many cabs per resident as those with restrictions.

Restrictions also inevitably increase fare levels over those that would prevail without the artificially created "virtual monopoly." A taxicab license or medallion in New York, Boston, or Chicago, for example, has in recent years cost a new owner in the range of $10,000 to $30,000. This cost is passed on to the passenger; it reduces the numbers of people who can afford to take cabs, and that increases the fare for those who do and invariably lowers the available supply of taxicabs.

Fare structures are important, too. Washington, D.C., for example, uses a fixed-zone fare system and does not permit higher fares to be charged during rush hours, when traffic delays clearly cause the operator's expenses to increase. As a result, there are from 40 to 60 per cent more cabs on the streets during off-peak hours than there are during peak periods, when they are most needed.

In some cities, notably New York and Pittsburgh, illegal taxis or jitneys now operate and legal taxis operate illegally, meeting a demand well beyond the "legalized supply." This is especially so in poorer neighborhoods and in areas without reasonable bus or subway services, and it is additional evidence that the supply of taxicabs is artificially reduced by licensing and fleet restrictions. The existence of highly competitive and fairly inexpensive rental car services in some parts of the country (for example, Los Angeles) may also be a consequence of the low supply and high cost of taxis.

Indeed, there is persuasive evidence that the public could and would support far more taxicabs than are now licensed to operate in most cities. Even with current restrictions and diseconomies, taxi patronage is holding its own while other transit services decline.

Statistics from Chicago, Boston, Pittsburgh, and New York suggest that already certain groups are heavy users of taxi service. In Chicago, about 45 per cent of all cab trips by residents are made by housewives; about 55 per cent of these taxi passengers did not have drivers' permits. In Pittsburgh, 60 per cent of residents' legal cab journeys are made by housewives, students, unemployed, retired, or incapacitated; 42 per cent of cab users are nondrivers, and 52 per cent say their immediate families do not own automobiles. In both Chicago and Pittsburgh, over 70 per cent of the female riders are nondrivers; for male Pittsburgh riders about 48 per cent are nondrivers. In Boston, households with low incomes contribute about a fifth of the taxi revenues; car-owning families with incomes under $5,000 use cabs about as often as those with incomes greater than $10,000. Forty per cent of the households in New York's Central Brooklyn Model Cities area with annual incomes of $5,000 or less account for 43 per cent of the cab trips generated by that area; 72 per cent of the area's cab riders come from households without autos and 85 per cent of the area's taxi trips are made in non-medallion livery vehicles.

It is my view that changes in taxi regulation, pricing, and operation would markedly improve the availability, usage, and financial viability of cabs and probably do more than any other transit improvement to lure commuters out of cars and increase total transit patronage.

There are three major reasons for these conclusions:

1 The taxi can offer the quality of door-to-door service which is competitive with, if not better than, the private automobile, because the passenger rids himself at once of both the burden of driving and the nuisance of hunting for a parking space.

2 The larger urban travel market, that which is diffused throughout the urban region rather than focused on the downtown and other core areas, is better served by a mobile, adaptable, accessible, and smaller-capacity taxi or shared-cab service than by bus or rail transit facilities.

3 The taxicab has real advantages over other modes as a transportation service for the poor, handicapped, and elderly. The poor live predominantly in areas just outside the cores of central cities, the areas increasingly neglected by rail and other transit systems now being built, extended, or proposed; the cab suits the needs of the handicapped and elderly, who require door-to-door service and should not endure strap-hanging and panic stops.

What conditions could be established to permit taxicabs to realize the larger role in urban transit which this analysis suggests they could have? Several changes in present operating conditions and regulations are necessary.

One necessary condition is the lifting of barriers on the number of taxicabs which may be operated in any city, and on the places within metropolitan areas where certain cabs may receive passengers. These restrictions now assure high prices and frustration for taxicab customers.

Regulations covering group and shared-cab rides should be re-examined. There are obvious economies per passenger when two or more people travel together between common origin and destination, and rates should reflect them. Such pooling would seem to be in the public, passenger, and operator interest. There are at present no general policies on these questions. Some cities allow an extra charge per additional passenger; in others, meter fares govern the cost no matter how many passengers are in the cab. Some cities altogether forbid a driver to pick up additional passengers once a fare is in the cab; others permit the practice during rush hours or emergencies and at specified terminals. During World War II, shared-cab riding flourished in Washington, D.C., and it has had a modest recent revival there. Indeed, during World War II and for a period thereafter, Washington taxicabs were allowed to display destination or route signs in their windows, a practice which requires no exotic technology or imagination, allows people to hail cabs which suit them, and reduces "hunting" for extra riders (and the concomitant starting and stopping delays). The dropping of shared-cab restrictions, the use of destination or route signs, and adjustments of rates to provide financial incentives to sharing for both drivers and passengers, could lead to far wider taxi availability and to better "car-pooling" arrangements than most people can now make.

We should consider more carefully the type of system under which fares are set. There are precedents for fixed-zone fares and for distance-based systems (with or without a time differential), and both have their advantages.

With a zone system, gerrymandering of zone lines can be a problem, and fares never can be matched exactly to the time or distance involved in a trip. On the other hand, passengers know in advance what the charges will be and thus can better assess the alternatives: walking, bus, or subway. And drivers have an incentive that works to everybody's advantage—they take the shortest and fastest routes.

Metered fares introduce variables and tempt drivers to use circuitous routes, but they may more nearly correspond to the real cost of a trip. New York City taxi meters register both the distance traveled and the time required to travel a given distance; as cab speeds fall below a specified limit, meters tick faster. This has the effect of permitting higher fares during congested periods and encouraging drivers to remain on the streets during rush hours. Common sense would suggest that taxi fares in all cities should allow a differential between peak and off-peak periods, whether a fixed-zone or a meter system is used. The differential would encourage higher utilization of taxis, lower fares, and increased patronage and revenues.

What about subsidies to assure that taxis reach their full potential with respect to other, subsidized forms of mass transit? If the arguments for taxis are good, then subsidies are not unreasonable. The precedent for free or reduced fares for cab trips for the elderly and for school children already exists in many bus systems; such subsidies would not represent a drastic wrench in public transportation policy. If wider subsidies are considered, there is at least the justification that such subsidies would not be used—as subsidies often are—as a lever to encourage people to use services they do not want to use; they would simply encourage a trend.

It is difficult to gauge the net effect of increased use of taxicabs on other transit services, on congestion, on energy consumption, and on pollution; but one can at least make some educated guesses.

The number and patronage of taxicabs on city streets undoubtedly could be made to increase with major changes in government taxicab policies. The volume of commuter automobiles might be noticeably reduced, and a substantial number of private cars probably would be displaced, some being those of former car-poolers and some those of drive-alone commuters. Even assuming no net reduction either in congestion or in pollution, though some can be anticipated, the diversion from cars to cabs at least would reduce the amount of central core space that now is used for parking.

At the same time, increased taxicab patronage would to some extent come at the expense of ridership on existing transit services. But since transit services other than the taxi already suffer from an overload during peak hours, there is little if any reason to believe that public transportation as a whole—including taxicabs—would be worse off than it is now. In fact, both economies and service improvements probably can be anticipated. Roughly 40 per cent of the average taxi driver's time is now spent cruising empty or standing idle, and even a small reduction in this waste would lead to lower costs and more efficient energy use.

The most attractive aspect of a plan to give taxicabs a larger role in urban transit is to give urban travelers a wider range of transit choices. Except in a handful of cities, travelers are limited to just two transit options—bus and private automobile. A third choice—taxicabs—could be easily added, and the most compelling argument for doing so can be made by standing back from the urban area and asking what new transportation systems will best meet the most serious, expressed transportation needs and the needs of people who most need help.

Today, we are obviously devoting most of our public transportation planning to helping people who least need help. With bus and rail patronage steadily declining, with affluence and the desire for decent service increasing, and with concern for the poor, handicapped, and autoless growing, unleashing the taxicab is clearly the next move to improve public transportation in our cities.

Major References
Domencich, T., and Kraft, G. *Free Transit.* Lexington, Mass., 1970.

"Journey to Work," Report of New York–New Jersey Transportation Agency.

Kemp, M. A. "Some Evidence of Transit Demand Elasticities," *Transportation* 2, 1973.

Kirby, R. E., et al. *Para-Transit: Neglected Options for Urban Mobility.* Washington, D.C. The Urban Institute, 1974.

Lee, Bumjung, et al. "Taxicab Usage in New York City Poverty Areas," *Highway Research Record 403,* NAS-NRC Highway Research Board, 1972.

Meyer, J. R., et al. *The Urban Transportation Problem.* Cambridge: The Harvard University Press, 1965.

Urban Transportation Factbook, Part I and II. A.I.P. and M.V.M.A., prepared by Barton-Aschman Assoc., 1974.

U.S. Bureau of the Census. *U.S. Census of Population and Housing,* 1960 and 1970.

Wells, J. D., et al. "Economic Characteristics of the Urban Public Transportation Industry," Institute for Defense Analysis, 1974.

Wong, H. K. "Some Demand Models for the Taxicab System in the Washington, D.C. Area," Urban Institute Working Paper 708–39, Washington, D.C., 1971.

The Taxi: Transport for the Future?

an Richards
worked as an
hitect and trans-
rtation consultant
only in his native
gland, but also in
nce, the United
tes, Morocco, and
udi Arabia. A score
his articles have
eared in the inter-
ional architectural
ss.

Since the fuel crisis of 1973 there has been a notable shift of interest by academics in the transport field away from conventional systems and how to make them economical and palatable to an often diminishing clientele, toward systems which had hitherto been largely ignored and which fall between conventional transit and the private automobile. Called "para-transit" by the Urban Mass Transportation Administration (UMTA), these systems include taxis, jitneys, dial-a-ride, and others, and we are attempting here to prove the potential of these new ideas for both the present time and the future.

In the United States today the taxi earns more revenue than all other forms of public transport put together, carrying more passengers than rapid-rail transit and half as many as bus transit, at the same time contributing, often seriously, to the pollution and congestion of the city. For example, in midtown Manhattan 40 per cent of road space is taken up by taxis carrying only an average 1.3 people per trip, and in the entire city 42 per cent of their time is spent cruising empty. Fares, too, are high, an average $1.95 per trip, plus tip. Even so, in an estimated 3,400 communities in the United States, where no alternative exists, the taxi has to take the place of public transport. It is these and other factors which demand the updating of present taxi services—for example, by allowing more to operate legally or, as the exhibition shows, by a radical re-design of the vehicle. New kinds of taxi-sharing operations could also be introduced, possibly using larger vehi-

cles which could complement or even serve as the city transit system. One type of operation already in use, called "jitney," allows taxis to run on a fixed route, carrying as many passengers as space permits, picking them up or dropping them as required, and displaying a board indicating the route being driven.

The Jitney Taxi

Some of the background to jitney operation in the United States should be mentioned here because many of the present laws and licensing regulations, which restrict taxi operations today, grew from measures which the privately owned transit authorities brought about through legal action.

In 1914 in Los Angeles, along the streetcar routes, driver-owned Ford Model T's cruised picking up often five or more passengers waiting at the stops (fig. 1). Thus began a shared-taxi operation, named "jitney" (it is said after the nickname given to the nickel fare charged) and which within three years spread across the United States (fig. 1a). The popularity of jitneys was partly due to the improved service given to the patrons—who preferred the quicker and more comfortable ride at no additional cost to the streetcars—and the speed of growth of the operation can only be due to the latent demand for such a service and to the enterprise of the drivers, many of whom were out of work and owned an automobile. In some cities, such as Detroit and Bridgeport (Connecticut), jitneys carried as many as half the streetcar passengers at the peak hour, and by 1915 one journal estimated that 62,000 jitneys were in operation across the country. Seattle, for example, had over 500 jitneys carrying 49,000 passengers a day, which gives some indication of the contribution they made. However, the streetcar companies suffered considerably from the loss of revenue and restricted the continuation of jitney operation by taking legal action. Jitney operators as a result were obliged by law to take out franchises to operate and pay taxes to the municipality intended to cover the cost of wear and tear to the public streets, in the same way as the streetcar operators. In addition, laws were passed limiting jitneys to operate only on certain streets, at the same time limiting part-time driving. So effective were the various laws harassing jitney operators that by the end of 1918, four years after they first started in Los Angeles, only around 6,000 jitneys were running in 153 cities, and by 1920 they were virtually extinct. Eckert mentions three important results of the decease of jitney operation that are with us today:[1]

1 Streetcars led to a linear growth of development, radiating from the city center, and, because finally they cost too much to run, were replaced by buses. Buses ran to a fixed schedule on the same streetcar route—unlike the jitney, which did not follow a schedule but was flexible and which often, for the payment of an additional fee, deviated from its regular run in order to drop a passenger.

2 The introduction of the present law forbidding taxis from picking up a second passenger, plus the introduction of a metering system, does not compensate

1 *Ford Model T jitney shown at a streetcar stop in Los Angeles around 1914. Jitneys followed streetcar routes and charged a five-cent fare.*

1a

3

Jitney operation competed with streetcar operation and often helped reduce loads at peak hours. A Model T Ford is shown here operating in Manhattan, 1912–15.

Car-pooling as one of the solutions to urban transit.

Example of "feeder bus" transfer point showing Reston (Virginia) passengers changing from their subscription buses onto Washington service.

Atlantic City jitney service started in 1915 and now runs 70 10-seater vehicles along Pacific Avenue.

the driver for operating during the rush hour and results in a dearth of taxis at peak hours.

3 An incentive to use the automobile without filling up all the seats available. (Car-pooling is an attempt to combat this factor by reducing toll charges for cars where several passengers are carried; see fig. 2.)

However, some of the objections to jitney operation were probably valid—for example, that jitneys were not properly insured (in Los Angeles in 1915 25 per cent of accidents involved jitneys), and also that vehicles were badly maintained because the low fares charged never allowed for the depreciation of a vehicle which suffered a great deal of wear and tear. However, the fact remains that jitneys were able to give a fast and economic service as well as a highly convenient one, at least on the main roads, perhaps better suited to the kind of low-density suburbs which sprang up following the growth of automobile ownerships. In Los Angeles, jitneys were so popular that there was serious debate whether to disband streetcars altogether; had this been done, it is interesting to speculate whether the city would have needed to embark on quite so drastic a road-building program. What is unfortunate is that jitney operation could not have been channeled into providing a service which complemented rather than competed with the bus companies.

Today, in the United States, legal jitneys run in only a few cities.[2] In San Francisco they have been operating on Mission

Street since 1916, and 116 12-passenger mini-buses now operate on this 9.5-mile route. A 24-hour service is provided seven days a week at between 1–1.5 minute intervals, carrying between 10–16,000 riders a day, picking up or dropping them mid-block as requested or at the end of existing bus stops (fig. 3). In Atlantic City there is a similar service which started in 1915, when the 400 jitneys then operating bankrupted the trolley car company; now up to 70 vehicles operate at the same time, running at between .5–2.5 minute intervals along Pacific Avenue and serving the fluctuating numbers of tourists who reach a peak population between June and September (fig. 4). Both the services here and in San Francisco are run by a Jitney Association, which enforces the rules of operation, negotiates fares, and arranges drivers' benefits.

Illegal jitney services run in ghetto areas in the United States such as on Chicago's King's Drive and in several of the black communities of Pittsburgh, for instance in the Hill District where it is estimated that 4,000 jitney cabs operate, with 8.7 per cent of all trips made by Model Neighborhood residents for trips often less than a half-mile in length. While most jitneys in the United States were forced off the streets by the private transit companies, jitneys abroad often represent an essential part of a city's transport system, generally offering quick and comfortable service at a price between that of bus and taxi fares. In the Manila area, for example, they are called "jeepneys," although the original modified jeeps are now replaced by a 15,000-vehicle fleet of 14-seater

5 *Privately owned serv-*
ice taxis operate on
fixed routes in
Riyadh, Saudi Arabia,
and other cities; they
pick up and drop on
request and charge
one-tenth of the taxi
fare.

6 *Photo mock-up of a*
London taxi extended
to maxi-size to seat
six to eight passen-
gers.

buses, which compete with taxis and the city bus company and account for 69 per cent of all trips made (a 1958 census figure). In Caracas, in addition to the bus service, 6,000 registered jitneys (called "per puestos") operate on sixty fixed routes, with an estimated half of the 6,000 taxis operating a "pirate" jitney service during peak periods. Here it was estimated in 1966 that half of all public transport trips were made by jitneys. In México City, Teheran, Istanbul, and many other cities (fig. 5), jitneys account for a high percentage of passenger trips. At the same time a very different economic climate exists in these countries compared to the United States. Not only are drivers prepared to work for low wages, but a high proportion of white-collar workers cannot afford to own an automobile and choose to pay the higher jitney fares rather than ride buses, which are used by the poor. In Paris, licensed jitney services run along two more direct routes than the suburban buses, traveling faster, carrying up to seven passengers, and charging one-third the conventional taxi fare. In Munich, Germany, and Besançon, France, night-time subsidized jitney taxi services run along routes which the bus companies find uneconomic to serve. Recently the London Borough of Westminster has shown interest in running maxi-cabs, with up to seven seats, between the main-line rail terminals, allowing them to display destination and route signs (fig. 6). The Greater London Council is also studying with London Transport the practicality of withdrawing bus lines in some suburban areas and allowing taxi com-

panies to provide jitney or dial-a-ride cab services. Airport limousines in the the United States represent the same kind of shared-taxi service, except that they do not accept passengers between pick-up points. Studies of access trips to Cleveland and Philadelphia airports show that access by limousine is almost as high as by taxi, with 15.7 and 12.9 per cent of riders using limousines compared to 6.5 and 2.0 per cent using the airport bus.

There does seem a strong case in the United States for allowing taxi companies to expand to include a shared-ride operation, to reduce traffic congestion and pollution and to save fuel. With an estimated 3,400 communities with no public transport at all except taxis, there seems considerable scope for experiments to be set up which could subsidize taxi companies to expand their existing services. They might purchase larger vehicles of the kind shown in the exhibition. Reducing the tax on fuel (transit companies pay no fuel tax) and subsidizing rides would not only encourage travelers to leave their cars at home and thereby reduce the demand for parking, but also offer a low-price service to those who could otherwise not afford it.

Subscription Services
Alternative kinds of semi-jitney operations exist where pre-arranged shared taxis are used by commuters on a regular basis. Such a system operates in Houston, Texas,[3] where taxis pick up regular patrons from a number of out-of-town shopping centers and drop them at any one of three points in the city. In Hunt-

ington, Long Island, commuters use shared-taxis as a feeder to the rail system. Van-pooling expanded rapidly during the 1973 energy crisis and is now virtually a self-drive jitney taxi service operating on a subscription basis.[4] Here, an industrial complex or company purchases a number of micro-buses and "matches" workers who commute from the same neighborhoods. The regular driver collects the fares from the others and has a free ride and the use of the van on weekends as a bonus. An almost unique kind of subscription service started recently in Norfolk, England, where, because the bus company was forced to withdraw its service between six villages, it provided instead, partly through County subsidy, a mini-bus and trained villagers ranging from housewives to a milkman to drive it (fig. 7). The service, which will cost an estimated $3,000 a year to run, may be met by the fares collected. The bus company's service would have cost $36,000 a year.

Ideally, a jitney taxi fleet would be licensed to operate in various flexible ways according to the demand.[5] For this to happen, however, one of the key factors would be a change in present legislation which would enable taxis to operate as public service vehicles, allow them to display signs indicating their destination, and allow them to pick up more than one party of passengers. New legislation making it easier for more taxis to operate, combined with cooperation from the existing transit companies, could lead to jitneys having a useful role to play, as they do in other countries as part of a city's transport system.

Dial-a-Ride
Since the demise of jitney operation the shared radio cab has been operating in the United States in a small way for many years, and since its identification as a system worthy of public funding, the last five years have seen a phenomenal growth. Today over 50 systems, called dial-a-ride, are set up in 22 states. Dial-a-ride normally uses vans or buses seating from 10 to 20 passengers, controlled from a single dispatch point to which requests are telephoned. Instructions are given to the appropriate driver, who plots his route at the beginning of each trip according to the journey possible within a given time. Passengers may also telephone in when the bus is under way, diverting the driver provided he has space or time, and they are told when they will be picked up and are expected to be available within a minute after the bus arrives. Different kinds of operations can be run, depending on requirements or the time of day (fig. 8). For example, at Regina, Saskatchewan, the dial-a-ride service called Tele-bus is used at peak hours as a many-to-one subscription service acting as a feeder system to the express bus service, or permits transfer to another dial-a-ride vehicle serving another area and running as a many-to-few system at off-peak periods. Regular passengers, such as commuters, pre-book their requests to be picked up at their doors or they can telephone in at night to allow a driver to update his itinerary before leaving. Widely scattered origins and destinations make "many-to-many" operations often necessary, and this service is run at off-peak hours in Batavia,

Community bus service serving six villages in Norfolk, England, provided by the bus company and driven by the villagers themselves.

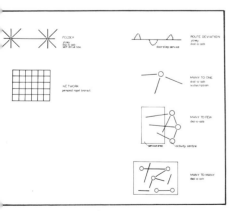

Diagram showing different types of dial-a-ride systems.

New York, with 23 passenger buses and ten passenger vans sometimes operating as jitneys along fixed routes and also providing a package delivery service.

Almost all the experiments made with dial-a-ride have proved popular.[6] In Ann Arbor, Michigan, for example, following a 2-year trial, it is intended to turn all transit operation over to dial-a-ride, and in La Mirada, California, 110,000 people were carried in the first year, more than double the expected number. Some dial-a-ride systems have replaced existing bus services; for example, in Batavia riders increased by 250 per cent over the bus services replaced, and in Regina by more than 200 per cent among high-income residents living in low-density areas.

Dial-a-ride offers passengers the nearest equivalent service to the private automobile at about double the actual cost of conventional taxi service. It is well suited to the kinds of trip required to be made in low-density residential areas, although some also advocate its use in high-density areas. It is only in the actual cost of the service that the problem lies, with up to a 50 per cent subsidy often required if fares are to be kept low. For example, an estimated $175,000 would be required to operate dial-a-ride in a town in Wisconsin for one year, using four 12-passenger vehicles with radios for a 60-hour week, and charging a 50-cent coverage fare with 25 cents for senior citizens. Partly as a result of these high subsidies and lack of sufficient support, several experimental operations have been withdrawn, al-

though in Ann Arbor citizens voted for a local subsidy to be maintained from a special addition to the gasoline tax.

However, the high cost of setting up new systems rather than modifying those that exist has combined with an interest in the role which the private sector could play. The cab companies, who were previously either skeptical about or who opposed dial-a-ride, have now prompted interest by the Department of Transport in allowing the private sector to develop dial-a-ride, and taxi operators are being given the opportunity to offer this kind of service for several reasons:

1 The existing cab company has more management experience than a newly formed organization.

2 Its drivers are non-unionized and will work for lower wages if they lease vehicles and are given the incentive to work on a self-employed basis.

3 The company and its drivers know the area already and will have built up operating experience.

There are at present a few companies operating dial-a-ride without a subsidy. The Royal Cab Company at Davenport, Iowa, has run a service for 40 years in competition with the bus service and without subsidy. Twenty-three 7-seater Checker cabs are used running 24 hours a day, seven days a week, delivering Western Union telegrams, carrying parcels and light freight, and covering an area of 20 square miles. An average 1,200 passengers a day are carried for an average $1.03 fare. The second unsubsidized company, The Badger Cab Company in Madison, Wisconsin, started as a jitney service, but when this was abolished it started a dial-a-ride service in 1933. Badger now operates 25 cabs in direct competition with two other cab companies and a subsidized bus service, charging the first passenger 55 cents and subsequent passengers 30 cents, half that of the conventional taxi fare.

Both companies use either Checker cabs or large automobiles, and believe they can operate a quicker, more economic service with this kind of vehicle than with a bus. Other authorities, such as Regina's Transit Company, prefer to use two types of vehicle—a 23-passenger mini-bus, and an adapted 16-passenger camper van—to allow for different capacity needs. Subsidies for the purchase of maxi-cabs would, however, interest potential dial-a-ride operators, as would a tax reduction on fuel. As the fleet expanded, subsidies could be given toward the purchase of more sophisticated radio-control equipment, and it is now generally accepted that while a dispatcher can handle up to 100 requests an hour, and up to 20 vehicles, above that number a computer could usefully be employed to deal with automated scheduling and dispatching—the drivers being equipped with teleprinters. Operators, however, are now very aware of the dangers, and cost, of introducing over-elaborate equipment before it is really necessary.

Finally, there is the question of physical planning around dial-a-ride. A low-density area will always be expensive to serve by any transport system except the personally owned automobile or cycle, but by accepting dial-a-ride as a way of life at least road layouts can be designed to help a system such as this. Drivers prefer to make a continuous journey without having to turn around too often. If dial-a-ride can pass at least one window of each house served, the vehicle can be seen by a waiting client, sitting in the comfort of his home. The clustering of activity around a transfer point— shops, library, and clubroom, all within a short, weather-protected walk of one another—increases the acceptability of the system. At Regina the dial-a-ride point was set up at a shopping center and proved popular with customers and retailers alike. A community consciously planned around transit, rather than the automobile, will correspondingly reduce parking needs and will avoid surrounding each facility with acres of ground-level parking, which militates against the pedestrian environment. Such transit will provide mobility to young and old, the non-drivers, and particularly the handicapped. The comments of a California administrator at a recent dial-a-ride conference sum it up well: "It is ridiculous to be building swimming pools in parks and not have ways for people to get to them . . . transit is another municipal service."

Once the serious legal barriers which now rule out shared-taxi operation are removed, we can expect improved and extended taxi services subsidized from public funds to be available, either to complement or run as alternatives to the conventional transit system at comparable fares.

9 *Two-seater electric self-drive taxi, called a Witkar, operating in Amsterdam, where Witkars carry around five hundred people weekly between stations.*

10 *Five Witkar stations*
10a *are operating in Amsterdam where ten electric taxis can park, be recharged, and used by club members.*

No article on taxis would be complete, however, without reference to two future developments, the self-drive taxi and the automatic taxi, both of which have been the subject of considerable public interest.

The Self-Drive Taxi
The concept of a small non-polluting city car which can be hired for short-term use has been around for many years, and the subject of research sponsored by the Department of Transportation and the Department of Housing and Urban Development. Three areas of study were explored:

1 To act as feeder systems to rapid transit.
2 To use in low-income residential areas.
3 To use in city centers.

Computer simulations which tested the feasibility of the system, carried out in Minneapolis, found that stations holding 18 to 20 cars could serve an area expected to generate 54 trips during the morning peak hour, such as might be found in four blocks in a low-density area or one in a high-density neighborhood. Redistribution by drivers linking five cars together was suggested, and the results of the simulation looked encouraging. No actual experiments have been made in the U.S., however; only hardware comprising a mini-car and an automated hiring system has been projected.

In Europe two experiments have been conducted, one of which is still operating.[7]

In 1972, in Montpellier in the South of France—a town of 170,000 people—a private company, Société Procotop, part-ly aided by government funds, operated 37 standard Simca autos with special slot machines attached to their dashboard. Members, on payment of a fee ($8.40), received a numbered ignition key and purchased plastic tokens which were inserted into the slot machine and "eaten" in transit, giving the driver the use of the car at a cost of 18 cents per mile. Technically the experiment was successful, although the average daily mileage of the vehicles would have needed to triple to break even. Unfortunately, the lack of parking controls meant that drivers left the vehicles anywhere rather than at the 17 designated parking places, making them difficult for other members to find.

The second experiment has been running for two years in Amsterdam,[8] the Witkar (or White Car), due to the efforts of an engineer, Lund Schimmelpenninck, who was also responsible for the "White Bike Plan" of 1966 which tried to introduce free bicycles into the city (fig. 9). This system uses electrically propelled 2-seater cars with space for baggage, which are picked up from any one of five curb-side stations. Each station has space for ten cars where automatic recharging takes place (fig. 10, 10a). The 3,500 club members, each of whom pays an entry fee of 50 guilders ($16), are given an electronically coded membership card. A member goes to his nearest Witkar station, inserts his card in the selection pole, and dials his required destination. The central computer checks that the member's account is in credit and if parking is available; than a car key is issued or an alternative station is indicated. The first car in line is taken and driven off, while the remaining cars move up automatically. On arrival at the station the member leaves his key, and the computer is signaled that the hire is over. Charges are made on a time basis of around five U.S. cents per minute, and the member's Post Office Giro account is debited monthly.

At the time of writing, this is the only operating self-drive taxi system in the world and is carrying around 500 people weekly. The continuation of this system, which enjoys no financial aid or encouragement from the City Council, represents a triumph for the organizers. The eventual plan is to extend the system to 1,000 Witkars, so that no point within the city center would be more than 300 yards from the 150 stations.

At present in the United States there is no apparent market for self-drive taxis because of the lack of incentive for their use. However, if special parking facilities were provided in city centers and more reserve limits were placed on curbside parking, this could change. The other potential could be in the more compact resort areas, or in communities where a small, cheap vehicle like a golfcart could be hired by the hour for shopping or leisure trips.

The automatic taxi
One of the most critical aspects of taxi and dial-a-ride operation is the high cost of drivers' wages; around 45 per cent of total vehicle operation costs; with conventional dial-a-ride using union drivers at around 70 per cent. Ten years ago when labor costs were soaring and un-

11 *Government-spon-*
11a *sored Cabinentaxi*
11b *system under trial in Germany:*
a) Plan of suggested network for Hagen, Westphalia; b) photograph showing station and cabins running above and below guideways; c) a 3-seater cabin being summoned by passengers at a station.

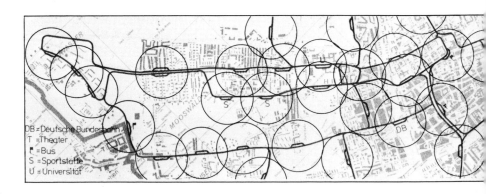

employment was low, efforts by transportation experts, notably at Stamford Research Institute, were directed toward finding solutions to this particular aspect of public transport operation: the reduction of staff costs through automation. Subsequently, proposals were published in a book *Tomorrow's Transportation* by the Department of Housing and Urban Development in 1968. This showed how improvements could be made to existing transport together with the development of a range of new systems, among them dial-a-ride and personal rapid transit.

Personal rapid transit or PRT consists of small electrically propelled vehicles running on their exclusive right of way, under computer control. Passengers walk to their nearest station, situated at close intervals along a network of guideways, enter a vehicle waiting at the station platform, select which station they require, and are carried there automatically with no intermediate stops. This concept, called by one British developer "Automatic Taxi," has come from the realm of science fiction to one where it is now possible to ride on operational test tracks in Germany, France, and Japan[9] (fig. 11, 11a, 11b). In the United States, two manufacturers, Rohr and TTI-Otis, exhibited systems at Washington's Expo in 1972, sponsored by the Department of Transportation. Many features of PRT are extremely attractive:

1 Vehicles of mini-car size carrying 2–4 people afford passengers a "personal" system with a high degree of comfort.

2 Lightweight guideways of small cross-sections elevated above streets or sidewalks would be accepted visually and be of low cost, making close-mesh networks at half-mile intervals possible (elevated guideways are normally assumed, although if rights of way were available they could run in cuttings).

3 Close station-spacing with off-line platforms and close-mesh networks could mean a maximum five-minute walk to or from any point within a city boundary.

A strong argument for personal rapid transit was made by the Aerospace Corporation of California in 1973 in a theoretical study for Los Angeles. A 638-mile one-way system with 1,084 stations was estimated to cost $1.76 billion, compared to rapid-transit's 116-mile system with 62 stations estimated to cost $3.4 billion. The system was estimated to attract three to five times as many people as would a conventional railway, with none of the problems now being experienced by the BART line in the Bay Region, where an average station spacing is two miles in the residential areas. This is too far apart for many people to walk to or from, and they rely on "kiss and ride" or sufficient car parking being available, as well as good feeder bus or taxi systems. PRT does appear to have many advantages over conventional rapid transit, although its critics present formidable arguments against it, some of which should be mentioned:[10]

1 Cost estimates for any new system are unreliable. A large-cabin PRT-type

system under trial at Morgantown, West Virginia, was estimated to cost $18 million, while $64 million has so far been spent on only half the projected system (still low compared to the Concorde's $8,000 million!).

2 The number of people who will use the system instead of their automobile is uncertain and may eventuate only if gasoline costs are prohibitive or restraint measures on usage are adopted.

3 The maintenance costs for the electronic equipment necessary to control large vehicle fleets (the L.A. study proposed having 64,000 vehicles) would require a large number of highly skilled technicians and far outweigh the savings from eliminating drivers.

4 Elevated guideways and off-line stations may not be acceptable in quiet residential areas.

5 Serious social problems may occur with unmanned stations and driverless cabins.

Some of these criticisms have been partly responsible for a change in the direction of development away from PRT systems toward those where larger vehicles, carrying 8–40 passengers, are used and which can run at minimum headways of 30-seconds to one-minute intervals rather than the one-second headways of many PRT systems. These systems, now referred to as GRT, or group rapid transit, are of the kind under trial at Morgantown and in operation at Dallas–Fort Worth airport. Larger vehicles, however, demand heavier guideways;

in addition, capacities above 10,000 passengers an hour in one direction are rarely required, so that efforts are being made to simplify the system with on-line rather than off-line stations —eliminating the need for costly switching devices. Much more consideration is also being given to reducing guideway costs (often 70 per cent of total system costs), as by finding ground-level rights of way, and one recent study for Birmingham, England, suggested making extensive use of redundant railway track.

While limited routes for GRT systems are likely to be implemented in American cities such as Denver, where the public have already voted for having the system as part of a "package" of other transport improvements, it will represent only a small part of the city's total transportation needs. It is the PRT system, however, with its proposals for city-wide coverage, that remains the most forward-looking, as it would give total mobility for passengers between all stations within the network. The Japanese have already produced studies for PRT systems for no less than four new towns. One theoretical study shows how an entire town could be structured around the system, linked to car parking sites at the periphery and using vehicles carrying people (as does the Dallas–Fort Worth system) and goods, mail and refuse, with special vehicles for police, fire, and ambulance services. Were such proposals ever built, they could mean fulfillment of the dreams of anyone who has experienced and enjoyed Venice: mobility within a totally auto-free environment.

A Future for the Taxi?

With federal assistance for public transportation proceeding at around $1 billion per year, it is paradoxical that under the terms of the existing Urban Mass Transportation Act para-transit systems such as those discussed can be eligible for grants only if they are under public ownership, and privately owned companies cannot receive aid. Once this is changed private taxi operators, for example, will be encouraged to buy new kinds of vehicles which better suit their needs and expand to new systems of operation such as jitney services or dial-a-ride. But this is still only possible when changes in legislation are introduced and when restrictive practices on entry are phased out, allowing more taxicabs to operate when and where they are required. Only then will para-transit be able to take a serious role in serving the needs of the community.

1. Eckert, R. D., and Hilton, G. W., "The Jitneys," *The Journal of Law and Economics 15* (Chicago: The University of Chicago Law School, 1972), pp. 293–325.
2. Kirby, R. E., et al., "Para-Transit: Neglected Options for Urban Mobility" (Washington, D.C.: The Urban Institute, 1974).
3. Webster, A. L., et al., "The Role of The Taxicabs in Urban Transportation" (Washington, D.C.: Department of Transportation, December, 1947).
4. Pratsch, L., "Car and Buspool Matching Guide" (Washington, D.C.: Department of Transportation, January, 1975).
5. Farmer, R. N., "Whatever Happened to the Jitney?" *Traffic Quarterly* (Westport, Conn.: April, 1965), pp. 263–79.
6. Special Report 154 "Demand-Responsive Transportation Systems and Services Research" (Washington, D.C.: Transportation Research Board, 1974).
7. Bendixson, T., *Instead of Cars* (London: Temple Smith, 1974), pp. 227–31.
8. Richards, B., *Moving in Cities* (London: Studio Vista, and Boulder, Colo.: Westview Press, 1976).
9. Richards, B., "Developments in Personal Rapid Transit," *Architectural Design* (London: March, 1974).
10. "Automated Guideway Transit: An Assessment of PRT and Other Systems," Prepared for the Senate Committe on Appropriations, U.S. Government Printing Office, Washington, D.C., 1975.

Photography Credits
Photographs not acknowledged below were
supplied by the manufacturers of the respective
prototypes in the exhibition.

Automobil-Historisches Archiv, Hamburg: 122
(fig. 20a); 123 (figs. 21, 22)

Demag/M.B.B., Wetter-Ruhr: 156 (figs. 11,
11a, 11b)

Glenn W. Edwards, Santa Barbara: 30, 31

Fiat Company, Milan: 129 (fig. 29)

Ford Archives, Dearborn: 144–45; 148 (figs.
1, 1a)

Free Library of Philadelphia: 121 (fig. 18b)

G. N. Georgano Collection, Ringwood, Hampshire: 110 (figs. 2, 5); 111 (figs. 1, 3)

Thomas Van de Grift Collection, Birmingham,
Michigan: 119 (fig. 18); 123 (fig. 23)

Jitneymen's Association of Atlantic City: 149
(fig. 4)

Museum of the City of New York: 113 (fig. 7a)

Museum of Modern Art, New York, Helaine R.
Messer: 126

National Bus Company, London: 153 (fig. 7)

National Motor Museum, Beaulieu, England:
111 (fig. 4); 112 (figs. 6, 9); 113 (fig. 8);
115 (figs. 10, 13); 114 (figs. 10a, 11, 12); 116
(figs. 14, 15, 16); 117 (fig. 17); 120 (fig.
18a); 121 (fig. 19); 124 (fig. 24); 126 (fig.
25); 127 (figs. 26, 27); 129 (figs. 28, 30)

Neubauer Collection, Hamburg: 122 (fig. 20)

Ervin Poka, The Urban Institute, Washington,
D.C.: 149 (fig. 3)

Brian Richards Collection, London: 150 (fig.
5); 155 (figs. 10, 10a)

3M Company, Saint Paul: 149 (fig. 2)

City of Westminster, London: 150 (fig. 6)

Roger Whitehouse Collection: 133 (fig. 7, 7b)

Witkar, CVUA, Amsterdam: 155 (fig. 9)